BY HIS PATTERN:

A Devotional
for Needlework Lovers

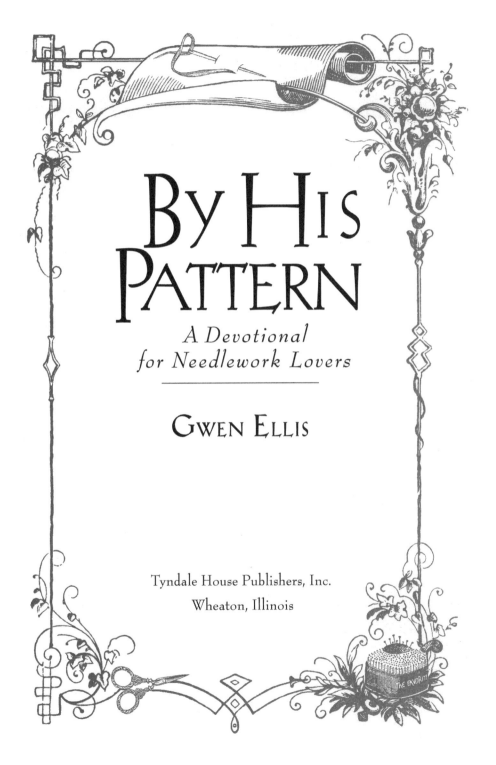

BY HIS PATTERN

A Devotional
for Needlework Lovers

GWEN ELLIS

Tyndale House Publishers, Inc.
Wheaton, Illinois

Library of Congress Cataloging-in-Publication Data

Ellis, Gwen, date
   By His pattern : a devotional for needlework lovers / Gwen Ellis.
     p.   cm.
   Includes index.
   ISBN 0-8423-4666-X (hardcover : alk. paper)
    1. Needleworkers—Prayer-books and devotions—English.
2. Needlework. I. Title.
BV4596.N44E44 1998
242′.68—dc21   97-35466

Printed in the United States of America

02 01 00 99 98
7   6   5   4   3   2   1

CONTENTS

INTRODUCTION / *vii*

PATTERNS FOR GOOD / *2*

WHITEWORK / *6*

CAREFUL CRAFTSMANSHIP / *10*

A DROPPED STITCH / *14*

THE TAPESTRY OF LIFE / *18*

A CORD OF THREE STRANDS / *22*

BUILDING ON A FIRM FOUNDATION / *26*

THE WARP AND WOOF OF LIFE / *30*

A STRAIGHT-STITCHED LIFE / *34*

A SAMPLER OF GOD'S GRACE / *38*

MAKING A MEMORY / *42*

APPLIQUÉD RIGHTEOUSNESS / *46*

NETS FULL / *50*

BLACKWORK EMBROIDERY / *54*

SOMETHING FOR GOD'S HOUSE / *58*

WHITE AS THE DRIVEN SNOW / *62*

THE LACEWORK OF A LIFE / *66*

A RAINBOW OF RIBBONS / 70

A SIGN OF HOSPITALITY / 74

THE TREE OF LIFE / 78

STUFFED FULL / 82

CUTTING AWAY WHAT'S UNNECESSARY / 86

A STUDY IN PATIENCE / 90

PASS IT ON / 94

WHY WORRY? BE HAPPY! / 98

SHADOWS AREN'T REAL / 102

BUTTON, BUTTON, WHO'S GOT THE BUTTON? / 106

DRAWN OUT / 110

WHAT'S DOWN UNDER SHOWS THROUGH / 114

MERE GOLD / 118

INDEX OF TOPICS / 123

Introduction

For the entrance to the courtyard, make a
curtain that is 30 feet long. Fashion it from
fine linen, and decorate it with beautiful
embroidery in blue, purple, and scarlet yarn.
EXODUS 27:16

In God's instructions to Moses concerning the tabernacle, you can see the value of fine-quality needlework. The curtains that adorned the tabernacle and the garments the priests wore all had to have an excellence befitting the house of God.

Through the centuries, needlework has played an important part in showing the customs of church and society. Beautifully embroidered tapestries during the twelfth and thirteenth centuries were a source of inspiration to those who visited the churches where the tapestries were hung. Museums are full of the costumed embroidery of the Tudor and Elizabethan periods of England. Quilts dating back to the nineteenth century can still be found.

From appliqué to quilting, there is a world of needlework techniques to explore. Are you a quilter? a knitter? someone who likes fine needlepoint or crochet work? Whatever type of needlework you appreciate, or like to do, this devotional can inspire you through daily readings on needlework techniques. Through it all, you'll get to know better the God who is the source of all creative inspiration.

Each day you'll find questions in a section called "A Stitch in Time" to help you think about what you've read and about what God is doing in your life. You'll also find a prayer you can use as is or as a springboard for your own talk with the Lord. Helpful needlework tips ("On Pins and Needles") are included to whet your appetite for projects you might like to try.

Are you ready? Then grab your work basket, and let's begin.

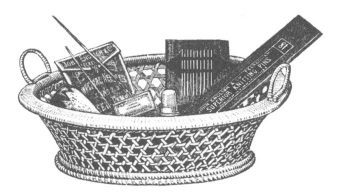

"My grandmother was an artisan of scraps, leftovers, and castoffs. She took what was given her and made something beautiful from it."

Patterns for Good

We know that to those who love God, who are called according to his plan, everything that happens fits into a pattern for good.

ROMANS 8:28, PHILLIPS

The most vivid memory I have of my grandmother is of her sitting in a sunny window, stabbing a needle in and out of a quilt held tightly by a large hoop. She was determined to make each of her eighteen grandchildren a quilt as an expression of her love.

But before Grandma could sit in the window quilting, she would first cut fabrics into the shapes she wanted. She spent hours cutting squares, triangles, and hexagons out of the fabric in a scrap bag at her side. I couldn't see what she saw as she selected her fabrics; some were dark, some brilliant, some the soft shades of evening. But she knew what she was creating. As she joined the pieces, she could see the pattern in her head and understood the need for contrast between the brilliant and the somber.

Grandma put bits and pieces of our lives into her quilts. There were the remnants of my first sewing project. There were scraps left after cutting a baby dress, there were tag ends of a dress, or a shirt, or an

2

apron. Skillfully, she joined them into familiar quilt patterns: Log Cabin, Double Wedding Ring, Grandmother's Fan, and Flying Geese.

The quilt she made for me (Dresden Plate) forty years ago now hangs over a banister in my great room. I look at it every day and think of the uneducated woman from the backwoods of North Carolina who created this piece of beauty. She was an artisan of scraps, leftovers, and castoffs. She took what was given her and made something beautiful from it.

Her love of quilting has created a similar love of the craft in myself. I have become something of a connoisseur of quilting. I make a special effort to see any quilt show that comes within driving distance. And when I'm at a museum, if there is a quilt display, I make a beeline for that exhibit.

I'm fascinated by the intricacies of the patterns, the miniature stitches, the colors chosen, the enduring quality of the whole project. I look first to see the name of the pattern on the card dutifully posted beside each quilt. Then I look at the fabrics used to make it. I marvel at the amount of thread put into the quilt. (This, too, is often noted on the card.) I observe the patterns in the quilting itself. I am intrigued by the variety of ways in which the quilt is bound; so, I study the edges carefully. Finally, I step back to view the whole, and the pattern emerges. The reason for the choice of colors is obvious. The way in which it is bound makes sense.

You know, our lives are like patchwork quilts too. When we view the pieces of our lives—joys, sorrows, health, illness, marriage, obedient children, willful children—often we can't see the pattern. We're so close to what's happening in the moment that we can't see the whole. But the Master Craftsman, the Ultimate Quilter, Father God, is at work. From our vantage point we can't see that God is creating something beautiful, but he is.

You can trust that God knows what he's doing and that someday he's going to let you see the pattern of your whole life. He will let you step back and see what he sees. Then you'll understand why the dark times were necessary to bring out the beauty of the whole person you are becoming. And you'll be glad you let him choose. ✤

A STITCH IN TIME

Which of the following phrases would you use to describe the pattern of your life: "bumpy around the edges," "stitching is coming apart"? What experiences led you to this conclusion? What are you trusting God to do right now?

PRAYER

Father, I can see only one piece of my life at a time. Sometimes I find it hard to trust you. Help me to see that all that happens really does fit into a pattern for my good. Help me to trust you even when I can't see a pattern.

On Pins and Needles

It's never too late to start quilting. Start with a scrap bag of good fabrics. One hundred percent cotton is wonderful for quilts. Perhaps you want your quilt to be all blues and whites. Fabric stores often sell small pieces called fat-quarters. These are one-fourth yard pieces for quilting. Watch for your chosen colors. You might take a quilting class. Start off with a small project such as a pillow or baby quilt to see if you like this craft before launching into a full-sized quilt.

Whitework

*"Come now, let us argue this out," says the Lord.
"No matter how deep the stain of your sins, I
can remove it. I can make you as clean as freshly
fallen snow. Even if you are stained as red as
crimson, I can make you as white as wool."*

ISAIAH 1:18

T he young woman turned back the layers of blue tissue paper, wondering what was inside this small package she had found in an old trunk in the attic. As she turned back the last layer, she gasped. There, cradled in the tissue, was a long christening dress of amazing craftsmanship. Tiny, white embroidered flowers and leaves cascaded down the front of the dress. Minuscule pin tucks paraded beside the embroidered panel. Lace inserts, edging, and trim had been skillfully placed and hand-sewn onto the garment. And the fabric! The thin, gauzelike material had not yellowed.

She lifted the dress carefully from among the folds of the tissue. She could imagine a proud young father carrying his beautiful baby daughter to the front of the church, the dress's long train hanging over his arm. She bent to observe each detail more carefully, marveling at the intricacy of the stitches. The flowers had been embroidered in white embroidery floss. Only two stitches had been used—satin stitch and stem stitch.

"It was your grandmother's," a voice behind her said.

She turned to see her mother standing in the doorway.

"Oh, Mom, it's so beautiful. I had no idea there could be so much beauty in needlework without color. And this fabric is so fine."

"Yes, that's whitework. The fabric is cotton lawn."

"Lawn?"

"Yes, it's a very fine fabric probably first made in Laon, France, hence the name, distorted from *Laon* to *laun,* to *lawn.*"

"Well, it's truly a work of art. I wonder how they kept it so white. If I'd made this, there would have been spots all over it from where I'd stabbed myself with the needle and bled onto the fabric."

Her mom laughed. "I'm sure sometimes the sewer did stab herself, but I'm also sure she tried very hard not to soil the garment because the stains were so difficult to remove. If she did get a spot on the dress, she would stop work immediately and remove the stain before it set into the fabric. If the stain set, the process of trying to remove it could damage the fabric. Hey, I came up here to see if you're ready for lunch. Are you coming?"

"In a minute, Mom. Let me put this back in the tissue. I'll be right down."

Once more she ran her hand over the beautiful fabric. Then slowly she folded the tissue back over the dress and laid the package in the trunk.

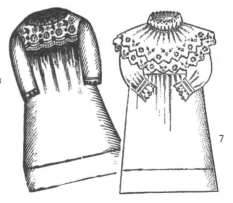

7

Closing the lid, she thought, *Someone loved her baby very much to make such a beautiful dress and to make sure that it was as white as white could be.*

If you're an embroiderer, you know the importance of tiny, precise stitches. You also know that the work can be ruined by stains that are left unattended. Many embroidery projects take months, even years to complete, and soiling is bound to occur. But the important thing is not to let the stain set.

That is true of our soul as well. The stains of sin—a little attitude here, a judgmental thought there—end up splotching the beauty of our Christian experience. The good news is that God offers the soap and water of repentance and forgiveness so that the stains of sin don't set in our lives. When sin stains set, removal can be very difficult. But God assures us that "No matter how deep the stain of your sins, I can remove it" (Isaiah 1:18). Forgiveness keeps the "whitework" of our lives spotless. ✤

A STITCH IN TIME

What would you like to tell God right now? You might have a time of prayer, releasing any needs you have. If you have a need for forgiveness or to forgive someone, why not take the time now to seek the Lord?

PRAYER

Father, thank you for sending the Holy Spirit to convict us of sin. Whenever I sin, help me to confess it quickly. Then wash me, Lord, and make me as beautiful and clean as a piece of whitework crafted by a master craftsman. Forgive me and make me like new again.

On Pins and Needles

Whitework has become very popular again. You might visit museums to see what people in the past did with white garments. If you'd like to try this, try to find the best fabric you can buy for your project. Use transfer patterns that wash out easily and won't leave blue tracings. You might find antique lace in thrift and antique shops to apply to the pieces.

As you work, use tiny floral or leaf patterns and work the design with only two strands of embroidery floss for delicacy in the tiny stitches. Remember that what you are creating is probably going to be in the family for a long time.

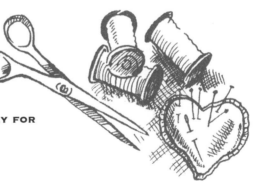

Careful Craftsmanship

*Work hard and cheerfully at whatever you do, as
though you were working for the Lord rather
than for people.*

COLOSSIANS 3:23

Hmm! What is this?" I wondered as I dug down into a drawer full
of fabric. I was at my parents' home in Montana and at my mother's
invitation was looking to see what kinds of handicrafts were stuffed
away in bureau drawers. What I had found were three matching pieces
of crochet with a rose pattern. The thread and the workmanship were
so exquisite that they took my breath away. I suspected my grandmother had been working on a tablecloth when illness and age over-
took her.

I brought the three pieces home and joined them with dark green
crochet edging and gave them back to my mother for her eightieth
birthday—a gift from both her mother and her daughter.

My grandmother was a simple North Carolina backwoods woman
who went to school only through third grade; yet here in my hands
was the evidence of perfection and craftsmanship. My grandmother
did not tolerate mistakes in her crochet work. She knew that if she

made a mistake and did not correct it, she would be compounding the error and soon the whole piece would be skewed. Although correcting mistakes was hard work, the final product seemed well worth the effort.

God's standards were just as exacting when it came to the needle-work used for the tabernacle. Everything had to be perfect, from the curtains adorning the courtyard to the garments worn by the priests. The "most careful workman-ship" (Exodus 28:15) had to be employed.

Fine crochet work, like any "care-ful workmanship," goes slowly, especially work as fine as the three rose-patterned pieces I held in my hand. Fine crochet work grows from the crochet hook a minuscule bit at a time. For most of us, some of the experiences of life are like crochet work—they shape our lives slowly and painstakingly.

In this day and age of instant gratification, E-mail, and faxes, there is a temptation to avoid anything that requires time and effort. The temptation to cut corners on a project that seems to be taking forever can be strong, especially when time is short. Nevertheless, we can still have the satisfaction of a job well done, even in the midst of these "do-it-now" days. How? By knowing that whatever we do can be done for the Lord.

Colossians 3:23 encourages us to "work hard and cheerfully at whatever you do, as though you were working for the Lord rather than for people." We can be "careful workers" in all that we do, whether we're engaged in fine crochet work, embroidery, or feeding the dog. This work ethic requires some blood, sweat, and tears at times. It

might even require a prayer for the patience to do and redo a project. But God is always ready to lend a hand. It's wonderful to know that when we ask him for help, he never refuses us. ✤

A STITCH IN TIME

Have you ever been tempted to cut corners in something you were working on? If you did take a shortcut, what happened as a result? What are some times when you're tempted to cut corners? How will you "work hard and cheerfully at whatever you do" this week?

PRAYER

Father God, you are the Master Designer. I depend on your help in everything I do. Thank you for the grace you give me daily. Help me to work cheerfully at everything I do.

On Pins and Needles

If you've never tried crochet, a pot holder is a nice starter project. Starting with a larger hook and thicker yarn (sportweight, rather than fine) will help you to see that progress is being made.

As you learn more about crocheting, you might make a sampler piece using many different kinds of stitches. Then choose projects that are progressively more difficult. After the pot holder, think about making a pair of slippers or a small afghan. As you grow in experience, you can start working with finer thread and smaller hooks. These are used in making edging for pillowcases and handkerchiefs. Eventually you'll be ready to try a sweater or a tablecloth.

A Dropped Stitch

*My goal is that they will be encouraged and knit
together by strong ties of love.*

COLOSSIANS 2:2

Knitting has been around for a long time. In the ninth century the
women of Ireland were knitting Aran sweaters—"fishermen's sweaters."
In those days fishermen's sweaters were coarse, heavy, almost water-
resistant garments. The wool of native sheep was hand-cleaned, washed,
and spun into yarn, but most of the natural oils were left in the yarn.
Thus the water-resistant garments.

Today Aran sweaters (called *jerseys* in Ireland) are much softer, since
they are worn for warmth and not in the rain. Now the oils are largely
removed from the wool prior to spinning. What has not changed,
however, are the stitches used in Aran sweaters.

There is a reason for all the cables and trellises in the patterns. Each
stitch stands for something and depicts a different part of Irish life. The
cable stitch stands for the fisherman's rope, and the trellis stitch repre-
sents the stone walls of the villages and houses of Ireland. The patterns
used are unique to each village. Long ago, fishermen who had been lost

at sea and subsequently found could readily be identified by the patterns of their sweaters.

It is amazing to me how much we can learn from making something with our hands. Knit two, purl two, knit two, purl two. It becomes a rhythm in your head. But sometimes, oops, you drop a stitch. Sometimes dropped stitches are an intentional part of the pattern. For example, when you want to make a buttonhole, you drop a stitch. But an unintentionally dropped stitch can be detrimental to the fabric of the piece. It creates a hole that you're sure to notice every time you see the finished piece.

As Christians, we are "knit together" as members of the body of Christ by "strong ties of love" (Colossians 2:2). A brother or sister who has fallen out of fellowship is like a dropped stitch. If we stand back and take a good look at the fabric of our fellowship, the absence of every brother or sister who slips away is a loss that leaves a noticeable hole. Each loss grieves the Master Designer.

Every member of the body is needed, just as every stitch is vital to the

integrity of a knitted piece. Yet sometimes we're tempted to think of certain parts of the body as more vital than others. But from God's perspective, every link in the chain is valuable. That means you are loved  by God and treasured as a valuable member of the body.

If we go back and look at the context of the verse above, we find a passionate spiritual father, Paul the apostle, yearning and praying for the well-being of his children. He says that he agonized for the Colossians. It seems that his whole goal in life was that the fabric of their fellowship be knit tightly together with no losses—no holes. ✤

A STITCH IN TIME

Have you ever felt like a "dropped stitch"? If so, how were you encouraged? Have you noticed that the "fabric" of your fellowship is missing a few "dropped stitches"? What can you do to share God's love with these individuals?

PRAYER

Father, I thank you for the value you place on the life of (fill in the name of someone you know who has dropped out of fellowship or who might feel that he or she isn't valued) and on my own life. Help me, Lord, to be a beacon of your light to all who need it.

On Pins and Needles

There are two styles of knitting: American and Continental. The American style is what is depicted in knitting books published in America.

When selecting yarn for a knitting project, check yarn labels for the dye lot number. Dye lots vary from batch to batch and may vary in color. It is better to buy more yarn than you need than to try to match the dye lot later.

Test any yarn you purchase for its recovery ability. To do this, stretch and release a six-inch length of yarn. If it does not return to its original length, the finished garment will sag or stretch beyond the dimensions of the pattern.

Most knitting patterns suggest the making of a gauge. The gauge helps you know whether you are using a needle size or yarn thickness that will fulfill the pattern's dimensions.

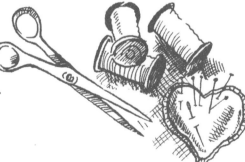

The Tapestry of Life

*Continue to work out your salvation with fear
and trembling, for it is God who works in you to
will and to act according to his good purpose.*

PHILIPPIANS 2:12-13, NIV

I walked down the long halls of the Palace of Versailles—long halls covered with gigantic tapestries ten by twelve feet in size. I had always thought of tapestries as dusty old fabrics with not much color and a lot of confusing images worked into them.

But this time I stopped to take a good look at them and realized that I was looking at the needlework of ancient women who made these beautiful hangings as a record of the events of their lifetimes, as decoration for the bare stone walls of their castles, and as insulation to help warm the drafty old palaces. Of course, the tapestries were aged-looking and not very bright; they had been hanging in smoke-filled castles in the days of the Crusades.

I walked closer for a better look at the intricacy of the stitches—thousands and thousands of tiny, fine stitches. I realized then why we use the term *tapestry of life*. Life is a tapestry made up of tiny actions, thoughts, words, each contributing to the building of a lifetime.

Today, when we talk about tapestry, we are talking about needlepoint. Needlepoint is worked on meshed canvas, and the entire canvas is filled with tiny stitches. There are really only two components to needlepoint: canvas and yarn. The canvas provides the sturdy, unchanging background upon which a creative design can be worked.

Know what? Christ provided the canvas of *your* life. He laid down the grid, the background, the stability, and the rules upon which your Christian walk is built. As Christians we are free to make many choices in the design of our lives as we continue to grow in Christ. In fact, the Master Designer encourages us to be creative. He gave us curiosity, a sense of humor, and more ideas than most of us can explore in a lifetime. He intended for us to use these gifts.

He wants us to explore the possibilities, to live our lives to the full so that they become beautiful tapestries of praise to him. After all, he did say, "My purpose is to give life in all its fullness" (John 10:10). He doesn't mind if there are some pretty exotic stitches upon the canvas of our lives. God has also given us a pattern to follow, a set of rules known as the Word. As we follow these rules, God promises to work in us "to act according to his good purpose" (Philippians 2:13, NIV).

A needlepointer could say, "Well, I'm not going to follow the pattern. I'm going to do this project my way. I'm not always going to work this piece from the front. Maybe I'll just turn this thing over and work it from the back." Although there will be no one to say he or she couldn't, doing so might create a mess that can't be untangled.

God gave us his rules, not because he is mean or unloving, but

because he knows the consequences that occur in a life without rules or structure. While the rules may at times seem confining, they *can* bring us great joy and peace when followed carefully. ❖

A STITCH IN TIME

How have God's rules and structure been a source of comfort or conflict in your life? What are the times when you feel confused about the pattern of your life? Have the choices you have made affected the pattern of your life? Think on the truth of Philippians 2:13: "It is God who works in you to will and to act according to his good purpose" (NIV).

PRAYER

Lord, I offer you the canvas of my life. Guide me as I day by day stitch the events, the attitudes, the spiritual passions that will give beauty and sturdiness to the tapestry of my life. Help me, Lord, whenever I fail to follow your way.

On Pins and Needles

You can learn needlepoint stitches within a matter of minutes. The only requirement is a relaxed attitude when approaching the canvas. The only equipment needed is a canvas—which you can get already imprinted with a design—a blunt tapestry needle, some good tapestry yarn, a comfortable chair, a good light, and some time to yourself. As with all handiwork, "practice makes perfect."

There's a simple way to keep tapestry yarn sorted and free from tangles. Take a set of plastic rings from a six-pack of soda. Fold each hank of yarn in half. Thread the folded end loosely through one of the rings. Hang the ring on the wall or just keep it in your needlework basket. Your yarn will stay visible and sorted, and it cannot become tangled.

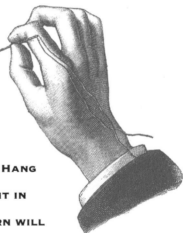

A Cord of Three Strands

A person standing alone can be attacked and defeated, but two can stand back-to-back and conquer. Three are even better, for a triple-braided cord is not easily broken.

ECCLESIASTES 4:12

I'm in the process of making my first braided rug. To be honest, I don't know what I am doing. It's a "learn-as-you-go" project. Since I have a very traditional home, and handmade rugs are so expensive and almost impossible to find, I decided to make my own braided rug.

First I decided which colors to use. I chose blues and reds. I decided to search thrift stores for good wool skirts and fabrics in these basic colors. The fabrics had to be some shade of red or blue or plaids with those colors.

The first thing I did when I brought my purchases home was to wash the fabrics and skirts in hot water to shrink the fabrics and make them even tighter and more durable. Next, I cut the fabric in strips on the bias of the fabric so that it would stretch and lie flat for a round rug. Then I purchased some little cones. When strips of fabric are inserted, the cones roll the fabric, making a nice smooth surface on the finished rug.

I started braiding, first with solid red for the center of the rug, then using plaids and blues. I found that the plaids added a wonderful color dimension to the rug. When I had quite a bit of braided cords, I started stitching them together with strong twine using a flat needle made for that purpose.

Why did colonial people use braided rugs? There are several reasons. First, three strands of fabric braided together become very strong and very durable. Second, they could not afford to throw anything away. Fabrics were too hard to acquire and had to be reused when no longer serviceable for clothing. Third, the noninsulated floors of their homes were cold; a woolen rug provided much-needed warmth.

A braided rug can be a visual lesson about the strength of three cords twined together as one. Although the verse above has often been used in the context of marriage, we can see it as a metaphor of the strength that can be derived from the binding together of Christians in a fellowship of believers.

We need each other. I need you. You need me. All of us will face crises in our lives. We need the closeness and warmth, the understanding and compassion, that only those who follow Christ can provide.

Those who try to stand alone in a time of crisis may stumble and fall. Can't you just see Satan lurking around the corner to see which of God's children is straggling behind? He attacks like a wolf after a trailing sheep. (See 1 Peter 5:8.)

The good news is that two believers can stand back-to-back, so that there can be no sneak attack. But the best news is that with two believers bound together *with Christ,* it is a cord of three strands that can't be

broken. There is strength in numbers and surety in the binding of three hearts. There is something about confiding our faults, our fears, our concerns to other believers and praying together that works. But the ultimate joy is knowing that Jesus is also part of our "cord."

Every Christian needs fellowship, especially when the hard times come. They are easier to face when at least three stand together. "A person standing alone can be attacked and defeated, but two can stand back-to-back and conquer. Three are even better, for a triple-braided cord is not easily broken" (Ecclesiastes 4:12). ✤

A STITCH IN TIME

What kind of a support system do you have? What are the times when you feel most burdened or alone? Whom do you turn to during moments of crisis? You're not alone, even though you might feel that way sometimes. You've got a built-in "triple-braided cord" known as the Father, Son, and Holy Spirit!

PRAYER

Father, I know that I cannot stand alone in times of crisis. I need your strength and the fellowship of my Christian brothers and sisters.
Help us to bind our hearts together in such a way that we are strong each for the other. Let me lend my strength to the fabric of their lives as well. Thank you for the gift of fellowship.

On Pins and Needles

When searching for fabric, don't worry about using dark fabrics. They can be mixed with brighter fabrics. The resulting rug will have highlights defined by the darker shades of fabric.

There is a device called a BRAID CLIP that has a pinching jaw to help you maintain an even tension on the braid. By opening the jaw and sliding the braid back into it, you can tug on the braid and keep your work even.

When joining the braid, insert a needle through the coils and pull them snugly together. The idea is to make the stitches as invisible as possible. It is best to work the rug on a floor where everything can be kept flat. Because the strips were cut on the bias, they should bend nicely without turning up and causing the rug to "cup."

Building on a Firm Foundation

No one can lay any other foundation than the one we already have—Jesus Christ.

1 CORINTHIANS 3:11

My friend unrolled several rugs and displayed some of the most gorgeous artwork I have ever seen. From that moment, I was hooked on hooked rugs.

"Tell me about making hooked rugs," I encouraged. "How do you do it? Is it hard?"

"It doesn't seem hard to me," she replied. "I've been making hooked rugs for a long time. First, I get an idea for a pattern. I might get it from a pattern book, a piece of wallpaper, or a china plate.

"Next, I trace the pattern and enlarge it until it is the right size. Then I transfer the pattern to a plain but sturdy burlap for the backing. Then I stretch the backing and tack it onto a frame to hold it taut for the hooking process."

"That part seems easy, but where do all these balls of fabric strips come from?"

"I buy old fabrics—skirts, fabric bits, and pieces, all of the same fabric weight to keep the pile of the finished rug even. I like white or almost white fabrics best. I can dye them the exact color I want."

"It must be a huge task to cut all these little strips."

"No, actually they are only one-eighth of an inch wide. I can cut them into uniform strips with this little machine." She indicated her size cutter. "I cut them about twelve inches long. That seems to be about the right length."

"Then what?"

"Then I take this hook and insert the curved tip into the mesh of the burlap facing in the direction I want to work the rug. With my left hand, I lay the end of the strip across the tip of the hook and draw this end up through the backing. I hold on to the strip on the underside and try to get the loops even on the top. It takes a little practice to get a nice even pile, but after a while it becomes almost automatic."

"Do you know what the most important part of the rug is?" she continued. "It's the foundation—the backing—the base upon which the whole rug is built."

Isn't it interesting that the part that doesn't show on the rug, the backing, is the most important part? In a building, the foundation is also the most important part. You can use the most expensive building materials, but if you put them on a shoddy foundation or backing, the house will crumble and the rug will fall apart.

Remember the story Jesus told of the man who built his house on sand? (See Matthew 7:24-27.) Talk about a shoddy foundation! The man who built his house on rock, however, had a firm foundation. We need to base our lives firmly upon the solid foundation that is obedience to Jesus Christ. We can do this through daily prayer and Scripture study.

A solid foundation assures us that our lives won't fall apart when the storm winds blow.

That's why the apostle Paul said, "I have laid the foundation like an expert builder" (1 Corinthians 3:10). This means avoiding spiritual shortcuts and quick fixes. It means hard work and discipline. If Paul had been a maker of hooked rugs, he might have said, "I bought the best burlap I could find. I traced the pattern on as carefully as I could. I prepared the materials in the proper way, so that at the end, the product would be beautiful and long lasting." ✣

A STITCH IN TIME

How solid is your "foundation"? What "materials" are you using to build on to your foundation? Why do you think using the best materials to build is important?

PRAYER

Father, help me daily to choose to build my life upon Jesus Christ, the Rock of my Salvation. I thank you for sending the Holy Spirit to help with the building process.

On Pins and Needles

The grid system for enlarging patterns is a helpful tool to master. Here's how it's done. Find a pattern you like— say, a picture of a flower you find in a magazine. Draw a 1/4-inch grid over it, or take a photocopy of the picture and draw the grid on the copy. Then take a large piece of paper and draw a grid on it with one-inch or two-inch squares, or whatever size it  takes to make the pattern large enough for your rug.

You can enlarge the pattern by drawing the design onto the larger grid freehand. It is slow work, but you'll end up with something that is fairly accurate to the original design. Using the grid system, you can use any pattern you find for your rug.

The Warp and Woof of Life

She has no fear of winter for her household because all of them have warm clothes. . . . She makes belted linen garments and sashes to sell to the merchants. She is clothed with strength and dignity, and she laughs with no fear of the future.

PROVERBS 31:21, 24-25

I stood entranced, watching an exhibition of an ancient weaving technique. A young Asian girl worked on a huge, primitive upright loom. Gossamer strands of silk as fine as a spider's web stretched from beam to beam. Slowly the intricate pattern of silk brocade grew under her hands as the shuttle passed back and forth through the strands of the warp. As I watched the shuttle fly back and forth, I thought of all of the centuries and all of the cultures in which women have woven fabric to make clothing.

Weaving is the most basic of the fabric arts and has two basic component parts—*warp* and *woof.* The warp threads are those that run lengthwise. The woof are the filler or crossways threads. So basic is weaving to one of mankind's most urgent needs—clothing—that we often refer to these elements as the "warp and woof" of life.

The woman in the Proverbs passage above provided for her family's needs in two ways: first, by seeing that they were warmly clothed; second, by earning money selling woven sashes or belts.

This woman was an entrepreneur with great business sense. But while she cared for her business, she first of all cared for her family and made sure they were warm and safe before she went to the marketplace as a businesswoman. And what is even more interesting is the description of her own clothing. She was clothed with strength and dignity and was able to laugh "with no fear of the future" (Proverbs 31:25). That is the picture of trust in God and his sovereignty.

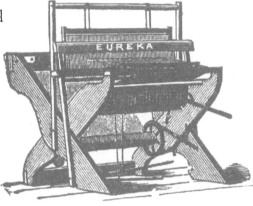

Knowing that God is in control of our lives helps us laugh with no fear of the future. The different types of experiences we go through constitute the warp and woof of life. Some we might be prepared for, while others are guaranteed to knock us off our feet. It's great to know that God is there to help us in all the practical matters. He has a master plan for our lives that is far greater than anything we've ever imagined. He wants to weave beauty, intricacy, dignity, strength, and courage into our lives.

Sometimes, however, we're tempted to take the shuttle from the hands of the Master Weaver and say, "I'll do it my own way. I have

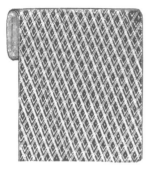

a better idea. Besides, God, your way is taking too long." When that happens, we wind up tangling up the threads of our lives and losing track of the original pattern. But Jesus can untangle any snarls of confusion if we're willing to put the shuttle back in his hands and let him take control once more. He is the Master of our "warp and woof." ❖

What concerns you about the "warp and woof" of your life? What "pattern" do you see emerging from the Master Weaver's hand? What do you need to surrender to the Lord?

PRAYER

Dear Master Weaver, I'm glad you're in control of my life. Whenever I'm tempted to take control, remind me, Lord, of your grace and forgiveness. Help me to trust you.

ON PINS AND NEEDLES

IF WEAVING INTRIGUES YOU, BUT YOU DON'T WANT TO MAKE A BIG
INVESTMENT IN IT, YOU MIGHT VISIT A CRAFT OR HOBBY SHOP TO
SEE IF THEY HAVE SMALL LOOMS. OR TRY TO FIND A SHOP THAT
SELLS LOOMS AND HAS BEGINNER'S CLASSES.

IF NONE OF THESE OPTIONS IS POSSIBLE, LOOK IN YOUR LIBRARY
FOR BOOKS ABOUT WEAVING. SOME OF THEM GIVE PLANS FOR
MAKING SIMPLE LOOMS,
SUCH AS AN INKLE
LOOM. YOUR MONETARY
INVESTMENT WOULD BE
SMALL FOR DISCOVERING IF WEAVING
HAS AN ONGOING APPEAL FOR YOU.

A Straight-Stitched Life

You can enter God's Kingdom only through the narrow gate. . . . But the gateway to life is small, and the road is narrow, and only a few ever find it.

MATTHEW 7:13, 14

"Olga, what is it that you are doing there? Let me see."

"Oh, I'm just working a design on this rough toweling."

"But you are only using straight stitches. And you've cut away the fabric between the stitches to make little windows. Very nice!"

"When I get a little more done, I will fill in these blocks with cross-bars and other fancy stitches."

"Where did you ever get such an idea?"

"I found an old piece of linen my great-uncle had brought from the old country. It had something similar to this worked on it. Since I'd never seen anything like it before, I decided to see if I could copy it."

Hardanger needlework was invented in the town of Hardanger, Norway. And while the conversation recorded above is fictitious, it could have happened long ago, for Hardanger needlework's lacy, open designs have decorated the costumes and household goods of the people of Norway for over two hundred years.

Hardanger is always geometric in appearance. It is based completely upon right angles and squares. Kloster blocks (blocks of satin stitches) reinforce the cut edges of the open spaces. These may be filled with lacy stitches of webs and wheels. The stitches are often worked along the edges of the fabric, which gives the piece a scalloped edge.

At first, the needlework was used exclusively on wedding shirts, blouses, aprons, and other traditional folk costumes. Later on, it began to be used on other household items.

The earliest examples of the technique were always worked with fine white thread on white linen. Some of the pieces were worked with so many stitches that the entire piece looked as if it had been created by crochet or tatting, since most of the linen had been cut away.

It is amazing that such beautiful needlework can be created using only straight stitches and by cutting away fabric. It is also amazing that a beautiful life can be achieved by walking the straight line of God's Word and cutting away the excesses of sin.

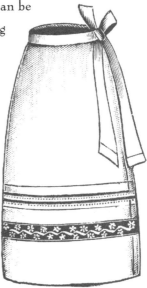

When viewed from the outside, the Christian lifestyle may seem narrow-minded and constricting. People on the inside may find it less than inviting, particularly when God takes out his "fabric shears" and cuts away the parts of our lives that don't conform to his standards. Yet within the confines of the rules, there is great freedom of expression, great creativity, and great exuberance for living.

Remember, God is the one who created the orchid, the peacock, the scarlet tanager, a world of bright and beautiful fish, and a child's wiggly toes. He knows what he is doing. We don't have to fear that his cutting away will in some way limit or diminish us. As God promises, "I know the plans I have for you. . . . They are plans for good and not for disaster, to give you a future and a hope" (Jeremiah 29:11). The snipping eliminates the useless and brings out the best in us. It makes those who view us wonder at the splendidness of a life lived in harmony with God's plan. ✣

A STITCH IN TIME

What do you see God "cutting away" in your life? Think about a time when God took the "fabric shears" to your life. How did you feel? How has God's "trimming" helped you in the past?

PRAYER

Lord, keep me right on track. Help me to walk the straight and narrow way, because that's where a beautiful life is created. Help me to see that the rules and regulations you have laid down are for my own good.

On Pins and Needles

Hardanger needlework is very beautiful and inexpensive to do. Visit a local needlework shop to learn how to do Hardanger, or look for books in your local library on the technique. Some areas of the country even have Hardanger embroidery clubs.

Buy the best materials you can afford. Hardanger, as with all handiwork, is time-consuming, and you'll want to produce the best work possible on the best materials possible.

When working Hardanger, use an embroidery hoop or frame and a fine tapestry needle. You'll also need sharp embroidery scissors for trimming away bits of fabric.

A Sampler of God's Grace

Lead me by your truth and teach me, for you are the God who saves me. All day long I put my hope in you.

PSALM 25:5

Hannah, you are now eight years old. It is time for you to start your sampler. Remember, I told you I learned at this age."

"Oh yes, Mother. Do let me start today."

"All right. Here is some fine linen and some good thread. And here, my dear, is your very first needle. Treasure it. Keep it safe, because there are very few needles to be had."

"I will. But what shall my sampler say?"

"That is for you to decide. Here are some verses you might like to consider."

So Hannah chose a verse and worked on her sampler for days, then weeks, then months.

"But Mother, I've done that stitch three times. I don't want to rip it out again."

"I know it's hard to keep doing it over. But would you want something sloppy hanging on the wall for everyone to see?"

"No," Hannah replies, then begins to remove the incorrect stitches.

"I shall never finish this wretched piece," she laments a few weeks later.

Her mother just smiles as she views her own sampler hanging on the wall and remembers her own struggles to finish it when she was a child.

Finally Hannah's sampler is finished and has been framed to hang on the wall. "Hannah, you have been patient. You have learned well, and you have completed a sampler of which you can be proud. And I am proud of you, my child."

If you've never truly considered the beauty of colonial samplers, visit a museum and search them out. You'll find yourself amazed at the intricacy of the stitches, the fineness of the linen or wool background, the evenness of the

stitches, the cleverness of the motto; and most of all, you will be amazed at the young age of those who worked such pieces. These were the learning pieces done by children who grew up to become skilled needlewomen.

The sampler served a very useful purpose. It became a library of stitches that, once completed, could be referred to again and again.

Hannah's story sounds a little like our lives, doesn't it? We try and we fail. We just can't seem to get it right, and we wonder how many times we are going to have to redo something before we learn the right way. We carry attitudes that hinder the testimony of Christ in us. We moan with the apostle Paul that we do what we don't want to do and don't do what we should (see Romans 7:15).

What's the secret to success? The same secret that little Hannah used to get it right. Keep doing it over and over until we learn not to make the same mistakes. Have a teachable attitude. Practice. Go back and start all over, if need be, until we can execute our actions and thoughts correctly.

I'm sure that when Hannah got in trouble with her stitches, she cried out to her mother for help. We can call out to our Master Designer to help us, too. In fact, isn't that what the psalmist is doing here—crying out for help, "Teach me . . ."? That's why the Holy Spirit was sent to us. As Jesus said, "The Counselor . . . will teach you everything and will remind you of everything I myself have told you" (John 14:26).

If Hannah throws down her work and refuses to do it anymore, she's finished as a needleworker. If we throw down the pieces of our broken lives and quit trying, we're finished, too. But if, with patience, prayer, thoughtfulness, discipline, courage, we go back to the place we made a mistake, figure out what we did wrong, and learn from it, then our lives will be samplers of God's grace. ❖

A STITCH IN TIME

How would you describe the "sampler" of your life? When are you most tempted to give up? What have you learned this week about the way God works in your life? What can you do right now to remain teachable?

40

PRAYER

Dear Father, I worship you for who you are. You are big enough to help me with all the areas of my life where I am weak. You are waiting to help me. Teach me how to accept your help and bring change in my life.

On Pins and Needles

If you wish to make a sampler, you can buy an assembled sampler kit. You might also check museum shops for designs and kits.

Many antique shops have samplers that look as though they are ancient. They have been made to look old. So be careful when buying what is supposed to be antique. Ask for some kind of verification of authenticity.

When planning your own sampler, consider using a frame. It will keep your work taut, which will make counting threads much easier. There are several different types of frames to choose from.

Making a Memory

[Jesus said,] I assure you, wherever the Good News is preached throughout the world, this woman's deed will be talked about in her memory.

MATTHEW 26:13

Sarah's wedding day had finally arrived. She looked stunning in her gown. Her headpiece was a cloud of white tulle. Grandmother Inga glowed with pride at this young woman's happiness.

"Here, Sarah. I have made something for you on your special day," Grandmother said as she handed Sarah a small package. Quickly Sarah pulled off the wrapping paper and turned back the tissue. Inside was a beautiful satin purse. "It's a bride's purse," Grandmother said, holding up the small purse. "See, it's a record of your life. Here is a ribbon from your christening dress. Here is a flower from your Easter hat when you were three. Here is a bit of your mother's dress for your wedding. Here is a snippet of lace from your dress."

The making and giving of a bride's purse is a tradition that began in the early 1800s and was the way in which the sewer of the purse honored the passage of the bride from childhood to womanhood and reminded her of her heritage. A bride's purse is small—just large enough to hold a handkerchief, lipstick, comb, and mirror. Each purse is different, because worked into the design are bits and pieces of a young person's life. Traditionally, the purses were often embroidered with the young woman's initials or a favorite saying.

It's a tradition that deserves reviving, because a bride's purse can be a reminder to her of her family, her traditions, and her values. Half the fun of making the purse is gathering the nostalgic material you will use and remembering the special times.

A bride's purse is not the only way to measure the memories we've made. Sometimes the things we do live on in the memories of others. These intangibles make up the "bride's purse" that is our life. Times spent with our children and special occasions with other family members and friends are fun to remember. Photo albums bursting at the seams, wedding napkins, videotapes, and other mementos are fun to discover once again.

When Mary poured perfume on Jesus' head, she was making a special memory, one that Jesus assured everyone would live on (see Matthew 26:6-13). And it has! Her generosity of spirit gives us a window into her life and serves as an example to follow. Although the disciples tried to rebuke her for what they considered to be a waste of good perfume, Jesus was touched by her single-minded desire to honor him. Now that's memory-making at its finest!

The things we do today become the memories of tomorrow. A life lived in obedience to Jesus and in the joy of his fellowship can provide many wonderful memories. This type of life makes a great "bride's purse" we can be proud to present to our Bridegroom—Jesus. ✤

A STITCH IN TIME

If a bride's purse were made based on your life, what kinds of things do you think would be included? What are the memories that are especially precious to you?

PRAYER

Lord Jesus, thank you for being part of my life. Thank you for the friends and family you have given me. Thank you for the memories, both bitter and sweet, that make up my life.

On Pins and Needles

Consider making a bride's purse. Sew the pieces together helter-skelter (crazy quilt). Press seams open as you go. When you have a large piece of crazy-quilt fabric, go over the seams with decorative embroidery. Lay your purse pattern on your decorated piece and cut around it. Cut the same shape from polyester stuffing and a backing piece from taffeta or satin.

Place the right sides together (stuffing and taffeta on the same side) and sew around the purse. Leave a small opening on one side, so that you can turn the purse right side out. Trim seams, clip curves, and turn it right side out. Finger press the edges so that the seam line is sharp. Fold up the bottom third and machine stitch the sides closed. Attach a snap closure.

You'll Need:

½ yard of heavy satin
¼ yard of several different laces (in beige, pale pink, ivory, pastel blue, or pale mint-green)
½ yard of satin or taffeta for the lining
½ yard of polyester stuffing (comes in a roll)
Ribbons and embellishments
Embroidery needle
Large snap for the closing
Sewing thread in a matching color

Appliquéd Righteousness

"Abraham believed God, so God declared him to be righteous."... King David spoke of this, describing the happiness of an undeserving sinner who is declared to be righteous: "Oh, what joy for those whose disobedience is forgiven, whose sins are put out of sight."

ROMANS 4:3, 6-7

Megan sat forlornly in the window seat looking out over the river. She'd blown it again. It seemed no matter how hard she tried to live the perfect Christian life, she just couldn't get her act together. She just didn't seem to be able to keep all the rules. She'd coveted her neighbor's new car. And she'd had a terrible attitude over and over again. She was just never going to understand how to be good enough to live the Christian life.

What Megan has not yet figured out is that none of us will ever be good enough to earn God's favor. God loves her as she is and is willing to help her become all he intended her to be. God's righteousness is something he offers to all of us through his Son, Jesus. We might say that he appliqués righteousness onto our lives.

46

The word *appliqué* is a French word that literally means "laid on." Fabric is cut into shapes—flowers, birds, boats, almost anything you can think of—and laid on another usually contrasting fabric. Then it is sewn in place either with tiny hand stitches or by sewing machine.

Appliqué is not a new technique. Appliquéd items date back centuries. There's a three-thousand-year-old appliquéd funeral tent in a Cairo museum. During the Middle Ages, appliqué was used in heraldic designs and on banners Crusaders carried. Early Americans decorated with appliqué designs.

Today when a needleworker decides to make something using the appliqué technique, she must first plan the design. There are three very important elements: color, form, and pattern. Each element is as important as the other two.

Once she has chosen a design, she will then search for just the right fabrics to make the design come alive. Fabric choices will be dictated by the intended use of the article. One might choose rich velvet fabrics shot through with gold threads for a banner for a church. But for a quilt, a vest, or a child's garment, sturdy cotton would be best.

Appliquéd and *imputed.* The words don't sound the same at all, but their idea is similar. An *appliqué* is something that is laid down on something else to enhance it. *Imputed,* which is used in the King James Version, is an old accounting term that means something is credited to an account—laid down upon it to balance the books.

Righteousness isn't a do-it-yourself project. If we try to appliqué righteousness to ourselves, we find we have added

filthy rags to our lives. "When we proudly display our righteous deeds, we find they are but filthy rags" (Isaiah 64:6). Not a very pretty picture, is it? Instead, we have to become the empty backing upon which God lays down *his* righteousness. We have to let him embellish our lives with the rich designs *he* has planned. Have you ever tried to lay down appliqué on fabric that has twisted into a knot? Not very easy to do, is it? The same thing happens when we try to fight God's attempts to give us his righteousness. We can sabotage his plan to work his design upon us. And what do such actions gain us? A twisted, wrinkled life that is not pleasing to ourselves or anyone else.

That's why God offers us righteousness. What do we have to do to get it? Just ask. He is faithful and will do more than we can ask or think. Isn't it great to know that his love is steadfast and never changes? ❖

A STITCH IN TIME

What are some times when you struggled to live righteously? What are some ways we sabotage God's plan for our design? When you feel discouraged about living a righteous life, how can knowing that God provides his righteousness help?

PRAYER

Holy Spirit, thank you for giving me your righteousness, which I gained through faith in Jesus. Help me to share that truth with others.

On Pins and Needles

Puckering is the greatest threat to appliqué work. Once it begins, it is very difficult to remedy the problem. It is better to take steps to prevent the problem.

You can prevent puckering by basting each shape through the center and onto the backing, as if you were cutting a pie. When you baste only around the edges of the shape, the center of the piece can puff up. Basting through the center flattens the whole piece and should eliminate much of the problem.

Using a hoop to keep the backing taut might also be helpful. As in so many needlework projects, if you see an error (in this case, puckering), stop and take care of the problem immedi-ately. If you don't, the problem will only get worse.

Nets Full

[Jesus said,] And when I am lifted up on the cross, I will draw everyone to myself.

JOHN 12:32

Many years ago, when I was a student, I spent a summer as a missionary intern in Jamaica. During that time, I learned about cast nets. One day while walking down the beach, I encountered a wizened old fisherman who had twisted his cast net into a turban and was wearing it on his head. It was a very strange headdress with little balls of lead hanging down from the edge all around his head.

I began to pay attention to other Jamaican fisherman and watched them standing on the shore casting their nets with a fling of the arm. The net would fly out in a wide circle and settle on the water. The lead balls around the edge of the net would then sink, and as the net was hauled back up, hopefully, it would be filled with fish.

It seemed to me that if the fishermen were not fishing with their nets, they were mending them. The process of making and mending nets is known as *macramé*—the ancient art of knot tying. It has been practiced since the time of prehistoric people, and it has always been used for utilitarian objects such as fishermen's nets and hammocks. As people became more civilized, macramé quickly became used for decorative arts. Ancient warriors went to battle with knotted trim on their uniforms. Ancient Egyptian tomb pictures show figures wearing robes with knotted trim. Assyrian sculptures show entire robes made of knots. And early in the Bible the priests' robes were decorated with knotted fringes and tassels.

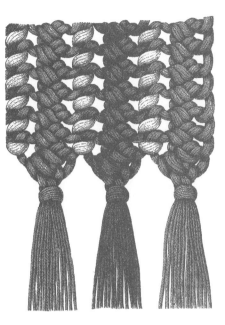

Without a doubt, Jesus' disciples knew how to "macramé." They were fishermen who used their nets on a daily basis. Nets have to be repaired, usually by tying knots.

I'm sure any fisherman hates to pull up a net and find a big tear in it. Can't you just hear the blustery Peter saying, "Oh, great, just look at that rip. That's going to take me two days to fix. *Arghh!*" But in the story of the abundant catch of fish (Luke 5:1-11), no one complained about the tearing of nets. There was only a plea to companions in a nearby boat to come and help haul the catch aboard.

Just think—Peter and the other fishermen had cast their nets all night long and caught nothing until Jesus came on the scene. Now here they were with a large haul to bring in.

When the two overloaded boats finally pulled in to shore, the Master

51

Designer—the Master Fisherman—had a new assignment for the fishermen: "From now on you'll be fishing for people!"

Fishing for people? That was a new idea! What would they use for bait? Jesus had that covered too. The "bait" was Jesus himself. All kinds of people would be compelled into the kingdom by his love. All the disci-

ples had to do was be available, to put out the nets, to teach, to preach, and to talk to those who came.

Like Uncle Sam, God is still looking for "a few good people" to put the nets out for the "fish." After all, fish can't jump into boats and crawl into the nets by themselves. The "fisher-people" have to put out the nets and wait patiently for the Holy Spirit to work. The Holy Spirit is faithful and will draw the fish into the net. ❖

On Pins and Needles

When choosing cord for a macramé project, be sure to select one that is suitable for the finished piece. For example, a heavy, strong cord such as sisal or jute is great for making a tote bag. Cotton thread is nice for fringes and lampshade coverings.

Bundle long lengths of cord by wrapping them around your fingers in a figure eight, then fasten the center to keep them from tangling. As additional cord is needed, pull another length gently from the bundle.

If you are working small pieces, use a knotting board and pin down the knots to keep them from twisting. If you are making large pieces, you will have to work with a hanging-free method. To do this, hang a dowel between two high-back chairs or use a spring-tension pole in a doorway.

You'll Need:

Cord

Yardstick

Scissors

Dowel

Rubber bands for bundling cords

Gloves for working with very rough cords

Ceramic-head straight pins

Knotting board

53

Blackwork Embroidery

*Fix your thoughts on what is true and honorable
and right. Think about things that are pure and
lovely and admirable. Think about things that
are excellent and worthy of praise.*

PHILIPPIANS 4:8

When my children were small, I would tuck them into bed at night
and pray with them. Sometimes one or the other would say, "I'm scared."
I was never sure if it was a bedtime-delaying tactic or if they were truly
frightened. Over and over I would tell them, "You just lie here and put
good thoughts into your minds." Then we would spend a few minutes
talking about something funny that their poodle had done, or about
some treasure we had found on the beach.

Through the years we had this same conversation. Their fears
changed, but the antidote did not.

The process of filling a mind with good things reminds me of the
embroidery work known as *blackwork*—an embroidery technique that
completely fills a decorative area. Blackwork embroidery takes its name
from the process of using black silk thread on white linen. In the beginning, only geometric shapes were used for blackwork, but later, other

shapes were introduced to the embroidery. For example, a pear shape might first be outlined in black thread, then filled in with blackwork embroidery. Once in a while, gold threads were used to give the piece a sparkling look.

In blackwork embroidery, patterns are repeated again and again so that the finished piece might resemble a very ornate wrought-iron grate. Although this counted-thread embroidery has an ancient history, its look can be very contemporary because of the use of black and white in geometric patterns. When completely worked in double-running stitch (the Holbein stitch) the piece becomes reversible.

Today this needlework is done on even-weave fabric with embroidery floss. Exact pattern repeats are achieved by counting the threads precisely. A fine, blunt tapestry needle is used so that stitches can be placed between the threads and not pierced through them.

You know, our mind is like the backgrounds used in blackwork embroidery. It needs to be filled in some way. We are given a choice each day: to allow our mind to dwell on the negative messages that come our way, or to think on that which is good, lovely, pure, honorable, excellent, admirable. Why is this choice important? Well, the Bible tells us: "For as [a person] thinketh in his heart, so is he" (Proverbs 23:7, KJV). In other words, we are what we think!

Let's face it—there is a lot of information available to our mind today. We are constantly bombarded with news of some kind through television, the Internet, office notice boards, neighborhood billboards,

 and magazine advertisements, and it's easy to have our mind filled with the unlovely. But if we consistently choose to think on things that are good, lovely, and pure, God's peace will guard our heart and mind (Philippians 4:7). ❖

A STITCH IN TIME

What goes into your mind on a regular basis? Is your thought life filled with things that are good, lovely, pure, and so forth? If not, what steps could you take today to change your mental diet? You might set yourself some goals to keep filling your mind with that which is good.

PRAYER

Father, help me to fill my mind with beautiful thoughts, so that when my life ends, I will have a masterpiece to lay at your feet. Grant me your peace, dear Lord.

ON PINS AND NEEDLES

IF YOU ARE FILLING AN EMBROIDERY SHAPE WITH BLACKWORK, TRY STARTING THE EMBROIDERY AT THE CENTER OF THE SHAPE AND WORKING TOWARD ITS EDGES.

TO AVOID A KNOT WITHIN THE DESIGN, USE A WASTE KNOT. TO DO THIS, TIE A KNOT IN THE END OF YOUR THREAD. INSERT THE NEEDLE INTO THE TOP OF THE FABRIC SEVERAL INCHES FROM WHERE YOU ARE WORKING. WHEN YOU'VE FINISHED WITH THAT PIECE OF FLOSS, CUT OFF THE KNOT, THREAD THE TAIL INTO A NEEDLE, AND WEAVE THE TAIL INTO THE EMBROIDERY STITCHES.

IF YOU WANT TO EXPERIMENT WITH COLOR INSTEAD OF USING ONLY BLACK, PLAN TO CHOOSE COLORS WITH HIGH CONTRAST BETWEEN THE BACKGROUND AND THE THREAD. THIS WILL SHOW OFF THE EMBROIDERY WORK TO ITS FULLEST BEAUTY. JUST BE SURE YOUR THREAD IS COLORFAST; OTHERWISE WHEN YOUR PIECE IS WASHED, THE COLOR (ESPECIALLY RED) WILL BLEED ONTO THE FABRIC.

Something for God's House

I will praise you, my God and King. . . . I will proclaim your greatness.

PSALM 145:1, 6

I was sitting in a large church just before a service was to begin. The decoration of the church was rather simple, which caused the two bright red banners hanging at either side at the front of the church to be very noticeable. Each was about ten feet long. On one was the likeness of a lamb, and on the other the likeness of a lion. Two people sitting in front of me began to discuss the banners.

"What symbolism do you suppose the lion and the lamb have?" one asked the other.

"I don't know," the other answered. "Perhaps it has something to do with the Creation."

I was surprised by their lack of knowledge that Jesus Christ is both the Lamb of God and the Lion of the tribe of Judah, but I was thrilled to think there was something visual that caused them to even ask the question.

Needlework has long been used to proclaim the greatness of God's acts. It had a prominent use during the construction of the tabernacle in the wilderness. God gave Moses specific instructions about the embroidery used in the tabernacle and for the priests' clothing. (See Exodus 26–28.) The temple that Solomon later built had workmanship similar to that of the temporary tabernacle.

The first-century Christians were not always able to worship in synagogues or the temple. Many were forced to worship in caves, where the only ornamentation was the sign of the fish scratched on the walls. But when Christians moved from their caves into rooms or chapels, they began to use needlework as an embellishment to their places of worship.

The Crusades helped to firmly place embroidery as an ecclesiastical expression. Pilgrims went everywhere throughout the known world, where they saw exquisite embroidery designs in clothing, tapestries, and other textiles. They carried these designs back to their homelands to adorn ecclesiastical garments.

The needleworkers who executed these designs became so skilled, and had such a variety of stitches, that they were able to create pictures as intricate as any painted scene. They used a technique known as shaded gold, in which gold threads were couched with strands of colored silk thread. If the overcast couching stitches were close together, there would be a lot of shading. If they were farther apart and more of the gold showed through, there would be less shading.

After the Middle Ages, the use of many forms of ecclesiastical embroidery diminished. Although embroidery has continued to be used in the church,

it never again reached the height of craftsmanship achieved during the Middle Ages. Perhaps it is a tragedy, since kneelers, altar cloths, wall hangings, and banners often were visual representations of the lessons of the Bible. Children, especially, may learn more from these visual representations than from the words of the sermon. There is something about

viewing a biblical scene week after week that leaves a lasting impression on young minds.

Since our bodies are also temples of God, we need to consider what visual reminders of Christ's rule and reign are posted on the "walls" of our hearts. As Paul wrote, "Don't you know that your body is the temple of the Holy Spirit, who lives in you and was given to you by God?" (1 Corinthians 6:19). Our soul can be a living banner of praise to the King of kings and Lord of lords. As David said, "I will praise you, my God and King" (Psalm 145:1). Praising God is a way to erect a banner and to show the world his wonderful works. ❖

A STITCH IN TIME

What is stitched on the "walls" of your heart? If a banner were made to depict your thoughts about God, what would it look like? What wonderful works would you like to tell others about?

PRAYER

O God, give me a fresh appreciation of your character. Help me, when I worship you, to remember you are a God of abundance. I want my heart to be filled with your praise.

On Pins and Needles

If you're left-handed, a good book for you to look for is Elegant Stitches by Judith B. Montano (Lafayette, CA: C & T Publishing, 1995). There is a whole section of stitch techniques just for left-handers. The trick is to use the middle finger of your right hand to guide the needle. The diagrams given are simple to follow.

Blocking and pressing are important to the process of finishing a piece of needlework. You can block on graph paper to check that the dimensions of the piece are correct. Place a damp cloth over the piece. When pressing it, use a padded board and toweling.

White As the Driven Snow

Purify me from my sins, and I will be clean;
wash me, and I will be whiter than snow.

PSALM 51:7

I grew up in sheep country—Montana. I am bred of sturdy stock and have a strong English heritage with a decidedly thrifty bent. And much like my not-too-distant ancestors, my family took what we had and used it again and again to save money and to provide warmth and beauty.

We did thrifty things like recycling old wool quilts. To recycle a wool quilt we would first wash it gently in cool water and mild soap. After it had been line-dried on a sunny, windy day, we would open the quilt and remove the wool.

By this time the wool might be matted and lumpy, but that did not mean the end of the wool. Oh no, not at all! The wool just needed to be carded to make it usable again.

Cards are a set of paddles with opposing teeth. The matted wool is placed between the paddles, which are pulled in opposite directions. If you do enough of that kind of work, you won't need exercise machines for the upper arms! When the wool is free of debris and tangles you then make a batt by reversing the direction and pushing instead of pulling against the teeth of the carding paddles. The result is a soft strip of fluffy wool.

Once the carder has a pile of batts—enough for a quilt—she can sandwich them between cheesecloth or thin muslin and fasten them in place with basting stitches. This secures the batts so that they cannot shift around in the completed quilt. This "batt sandwich" is placed between a front and backing fabric. Then the whole quilt—front, back, and batt filling—is tied together.

Wool is one of God's best gifts to mankind, but in order for wool to be used, it must first be cleaned. Sheep farmers shear their flocks twice annually to remove the thick coat of wool. Wool straight from the sheep is a dirty, filthy, lanolin-laden mess. It smells bad and it feels worse. Until wool has been cleaned, it is virtually worthless.

In Bible times, wool was cleaned by a tradesman known as a "fuller." The fuller used ashes and other alkalis to remove the gummy substances found on raw wool fibers. The process involved dipping, beating, washing, and then sun-bleaching the wool.

We may feel like that at times when God starts the purifying process in our own lives. It is an ongoing, sometimes difficult process that also happens to be lifelong!

Sometimes we need to be cleansed from an attitude or behavior that keeps us from being used to the fullest by God. Yet until we submit to the process, we won't be very useful, either. The good news is that provision has been made for the cleaning of the "wool" of our souls. We are cleansed by the blood of the Lamb of God, who died to make us white as snow. Like David, we can say, "Purify me from my sins, and I will be clean; wash me, and I will be whiter than snow" (Psalm 51:7). ✤

A STITCH IN TIME

What do you think is the hardest part of the cleansing process? How do you know when you're due for a "cleaning"?

PRAYER

Father God, thank you for giving me your Son, Jesus Christ, to be my "fuller." Help me, Lord, to submit to your will in every aspect of my life.

On Pins and Needles

If you have wool quilts that have become lumpy and worn, consider the possibility of opening them, washing the wool by hand in cool water, and recarding the wool. Some yarn shops have carding paddles that are fairly inexpensive.

After washing the wool in cool water, drying it thoroughly (not in the hot sun), and carding it into batts, arrange the batts on stretched cheesecloth. Cover the entire cheesecloth with an even density of wool. Then lay a second cheesecloth on the top, and, with large basting stitches, sew the entire batt together. Stitch first in an <u>X</u> across the entire batt. Then stitch vertically and horizontally at the middle of the batt. That should hold everything in place unless you are working with a very large batt. If that is the case, use additional basting stitches.

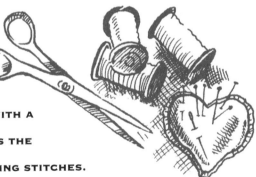

The Lacework of a Life

I was in an outdoor market in Holland watching a lacemaker in traditional Dutch cap and apron, both trimmed with what I presumed was bobbin lace. My mind was boggled as I watched her hands fly among two dozen bobbins wound with thread. How did she keep them straight? How did she know what she was doing? The evidence that she knew was the beautiful strip of lace steadily growing on the pillow. I could hardly tear my eyes away from her flying hands.

Bobbin lace is also called *pillow lace* because it is worked from a paper pattern, called a *pricking*, on a pillow. As the lace is formed, it is pricked through the pattern to the pillow with pins. Simple lace can be formed with a few pairs of bobbins. Complex floral or geometric designs can require hundreds of bobbins.

A bobbin is what the thread is wrapped around, and it can be as simple as a large nail or as elaborate as ivory. Traditionally, bobbins were made of wood or bone. They are still available today, and it is best to work with commercially made bobbins instead of some makeshift devices such as nails.

While threads for bobbin lace were once made of silk or linen, with some metallic threads used, today most lacemakers use finely spun cotton threads. Traditionally, the pricking pattern was of parchment so that it could be reused, but now graph paper is best and the design can be photocopied before being pricked.

Bobbins are always used in pairs, so that the lacemaker is picking up pairs of bobbins from each side simultaneously. As lace-makers become proficient, they can pick up and lay down the bobbins very quickly, thus giving the illusion of flying hands.

The good news about all this seeming complex-ity is that there are only two basic stitches: a half stitch and a whole stitch. While bobbin lace looks complicated, it is simply a matter of learning the technique and doing it again and again until the actions become automatic.

As the lacemaker works, she is looking at the underside of the lace. The finished side is being worked away from her. She may get a peek at the finished side from time to time, but the whole effect will not be seen until she removes the lace from the pillow, and perhaps attaches it to a garment. Then she will see the true beauty of the whole piece.

There are a lot of circumstances in our lives that don't make sense, because we can't see "the whole story." We find ourselves asking questions like: "Why didn't I have this piece of information when I had to make that big decision? I could have made a better decision" or "Why does God seem so far away during this crisis?"

Like the lacemaker, we are working our lives from the underside and can't see everything. The finished product is a mystery that won't be revealed until we get to heaven. God, however, sees both sides. One day we'll see the reason for the twists and turns our life has taken. Then we'll understand why the Master Designer led us in the paths that he did. ❖

A STITCH IN TIME

In what situations are you most tempted to doubt or question God? What do you believe about God's plan for your life? What do you need God to help you with right now?

PRAYER

Father God, Master Designer of my life, help me. Sometimes it seems that I have more questions than answers. My life seems so complex. Yet I know that I am your child, the workmanship of your hands. Help me to trust you.

On Pins and Needles

Bobbin lace is not terribly difficult to learn. After all, there are only two stitches to learn. Get a good book that shows you pictorially how to make lace. A great book with easy-to-follow directions is <u>Complete Guide to Needlework</u> by <u>Reader's Digest</u>.

A clothespin or a slotted dowel can serve as a bobbin. Check the pattern you'd like to try for the exact bobbin requirements. Visit a museum or historic site where you might see bobbin lace being made. Call local needlework shops to see if they know where classes in bobbin lace are held. This is a beautiful needlework that needs to be made more popular. It is an art form that must not be lost to future generations.

You'll Need:

Board or "pillow"
Dressmaker pins
Graph paper for pricking
Bobbins
Crochet hook
Pricker, scissors, drawing ink,
   yardstick

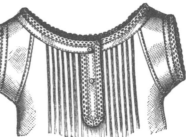

A Rainbow of Ribbons

*This truth gives them the confidence of eternal
life, which God promised them before the world
began—and he cannot lie.*

TITUS 1:2

Once, long ago when my children were small, we heard about
above-ground nuclear tests in the then Soviet Union. There were dire
warnings about radioactive material drifting over the Pacific Ocean
to the Pacific Northwest, where we lived. My kids heard the reports,
and they were scared—and so was I.

I had gone shopping on a typical rainy Seattle day and found myself
stranded in my car by a deluge. The sky was black with boiling clouds,
the parking lot was running with water. I waited for a while until the
rain subsided and then I made a mad dash for the store. I did my shopping and came outside expecting to have to scamper back to the car.
But a surprise awaited me: sunshine . . . and a rainbow—a complete,
perfectly arched rainbow, brilliantly arched against the blackness of
the clouds. A rainbow, God's symbol of his promises.

I didn't know what would happen when nuclear particles drifted over
our area. I didn't know about a lot of things that would (and have)

threatened our lives in the intervening years, but I knew then and am even more sure now that God's promises are true and that he has never lost control of any part of his creation. I could go home from that shopping excursion and tell my children that God was with us. I could offer them comfort and hope, because God is the God of hope. It was written there in his multicolored bow set against the blackness of the storm clouds.

When I think of that rainbow, I think of one of the most colorful types of needlework—ribbon weaving. Ribbon weaving is simply weaving a rainbow of ribbons. First, the shape of the finished project is traced onto fabric with a pencil. Then a row of ribbons is created by the insertion of a tapestry needle threaded with silk or rayon ribbon to make vertical stitches up and down over the fabric. When the vertical row is completed, ribbon is woven through them. At the end of each woven row, the needle is inserted into the fabric backing close to the place where it was inserted previously. That fills the weaving solidly, covering the fabric completely and allowing only the ribbons to show.

Ribbon weaving is nice for the tops of decorative boxes, lockets, or insets on pillowcases, collars, and pockets. It can also be a constant reminder to you that the Lord God never fails in his promises to his people. As God told Noah, "I have placed my rainbow in the clouds. It is the sign of my

permanent promise to you and to all the earth" (Genesis 9:13). Throughout the centuries the colorful bow has never failed to appear

in the sky. On that rainy day in Seattle it was a sign of immense comfort to me.

In a time when leaders in government and business don't always keep their promises, it is reassuring to know that we serve a God who does not lie. He keeps his promises. ✤

A STITCH IN TIME

When was the last time you felt afraid or lonely? Is there anything that scares you about life today? How can knowing that God doesn't lie help? Think about a time in the past when God helped you with a problem. How did he reassure you?

PRAYER

Sometimes, Lord God, I feel afraid and alone. When those times come, Lord, remind me of your promises once more. Help me to remember that you will never leave me. Give me your peace and confidence.

On Pins and Needles

If you use ribbon with variegated color rather than ribbons of many different colors for your ribbon work, there will be plenty of color in your design. Variegated ribbon might be a good idea for a first project.

If you are using multicolored ribbons, thread several tapestry needles before you begin. This will save time and make it easier to choose the color you wish to use next.

Tapestry needles, because of their blunt points, will slip between the threads of the backing instead of piercing them. If you were to pierce the threads of the fabric when doing ribbon work, it would be almost impossible to pull the ribbon in and out of the fabric.

A Sign of Hospitality

Don't forget to show hospitality to strangers,
for some who have done this have entertained
angels without realizing it!

HEBREWS 13:2

"Sarah, quick, bake some bread." A flustered Abraham rushed into her tent.

"Why the great rush?" Sarah asked.

"We have visitors—very special visitors—and I must tell one of the men to prepare meat for a feast."

With that, Abraham rushed out of the tent. Sarah hurried to do what her husband asked, but first she took just one quick peek at the visitors. *Hmmm, rather ordinary looking. And so dusty from walking. I don't know what all the fuss is about, but I'll do as Abraham asks. After all, hospitality is his hallmark.*

Hospitality has been the hallmark of many people throughout the centuries. In the early days of our country, the pineapple was a symbol of hospitality, and there was a good reason for it.

When America was new and few treats were available, once in a while ships would come to port from tropical climes and bring exotic fruits, one of which would be the pineapple. Since pineapples were rare and expensive, having a pineapple was a very special treat that was reserved for times when a host and hostess wanted to honor a special guest. Thus, the pineapple became the symbol of hospitality.

The pineapple is one of those wonderful designs that occurs in nature that is so perfect and so fascinating that our eyes never tire of looking at it. The symmetry of the plates that cover the body of the fruit, the bright-green, spiky leaves topping it. It is no wonder that we copy it again and again in our needlework.

Very early in our history as a nation, the pineapple design began to be incorporated into knitted pieces, quilts, signboards outside inns, newels on staircases, stencils for the walls, and toppers on the posts of beds, to name a few. We still use this pleasing design today, and almost any needlework book has at least one design based on the pineapple. I visited recently in the home of a well-known author who had on her dining room table a crocheted tablecloth done in a pineapple design. It had been made by her aged mother, who sat nearby and watched the day's proceedings. She was at home here, and so were we.

There are other signs of hospitality, some not as tangible as the pineapple. These signs are a willingness to serve, a heart full of love, and an unhurried attitude. If you are hospitable, you may find yourself entertaining angels as Abraham, Sarah, and probably a lot of other people have throughout history.

A hospitable home—your home—is a place of refuge, a place of peace and rest, a place where a person can relax and be himself or herself. This home need not be a candidate for the cover of *Architectural Digest*. It just needs to be a home where the Spirit of the Lord rests. When our heart is hospitable and open to the Lord's leading, our home will be hospitable also. ✛

A STITCH IN TIME

What is your HQ—your Hospitality Quotient? How willing are you to invite others in and make them feel comfortable in your home? How can you share your hospitality with someone this week? Whenever we're busy, the thought of having to entertain people can be burdensome. Know that small things, such as a smile or a friendly greeting, can provide as much hospitality as an eight-course dinner party!

PRAYER

Father, give me a willing heart about hospitality. You tell me to share with your people who are in need and to practice hospitality (Romans 12:13). Help me, Father, to be willing to open my heart and home.

ON PINS AND NEEDLES

THINK OF WAYS TO USE THE PINEAPPLE MOTIF IN YOUR HOME AS
A REMINDER TO YOURSELF THAT GOD'S DESIRE IS FOR US TO BE
HOSPITABLE.

THE PINEAPPLE SHAPE LENDS ITSELF WELL TO TRAPUNTO,
CROCHET, CREWEL EMBROIDERY, HOOKED RUGS, APPLIQUÉD QUILTS,
NEEDLEPOINT, AND MANY OTHER NEEDLEWORK PROJECTS.

BEGIN NOW TO LOOK FOR PINEAPPLE
DESIGNS THAT COULD BE INCORPORATED
INTO YOUR NEEDLEWORK, OR
ENLARGE THE DESIGN GIVEN OPPO-
SITE AS A BASIS FOR YOUR WORK.

The Tree of Life

Then the Lord God said, "The people have become as we are, knowing everything, both good and evil. What if they eat the fruit of the tree of life? Then they will live forever!"

GENESIS 3:22

Mother, what are you making?" little Lucinda asked her mother.

"This will be a covering for the chair we use for guests. It is a very special chair, and I am trying to do this very carefully."

"What is the pattern? There is so much color and so many things in the design. Look, there are birds and fruit and a big tree, and . . . and . . ."

Mother chuckled. "The pattern is called the Tree of Life, and I'm working it on this very fine linen with wool."

"It's lovely, Mother. What do you call it?"

"It's called crewel embroidery. Do you like it?"

"Oh, yes, Mother, very much!"

In crewel embroidery the best-loved and most-wanted design is that of the tree of life. There are many tree of life designs, but the basic idea always stays the same. There is always a tree rising from the ground that is done in graduated shading. The trees are exotic and have an abundance of life—flowers, leaves, birds, butterflies, and fruits hanging from them. The designs are always big and bold.

Crewel is also called Jacobean embroidery and was first introduced in England. The word *crewel* comes from *krua,* which means "wool." In the beginning, crewel embroidery was always worked with wool yarn upon wool cloth. Today the background might be of linen, cotton, or silk as well as wool.

Only a few stitches are used in crewel work, but the variations that can be created with them are many. The common stitches are chain, stem, long-and-short, straight or satin, French knot, running, feather, and herringbone, with some composite stitches used as filler.

The term *crewel* actually refers to the thread used. It is a fine, two-ply wool. Only a piece worked in crewel thread can be classified as true crewel embroidery. Fine imported crewel yarns come in more than three hundred colors, and in many weights. The thread is usually twenty inches long, since anything longer is likely to tangle.

Most often, the Tree of Life pattern is worked in colors representing nature. The pattern was probably chosen so often because it spoke of richness and offered many possibilities to the crewel worker. But for us who work crewel, the design can become a constant reminder that God drove Adam and Eve out of the Garden of Eden

after their sin, so that they would not eat of the genuine tree of life and live forever. It can also remind us of another tree of life.

The Bible refers to Jesus Christ as the second Adam. The first Adam  brought us sin and death by his actions. The second Adam brought us life—eternal life—by his actions. And both sets of actions occurred at a tree. The first Adam sinned at the tree of life. On a tree of crucifixion, the second Adam bought redemption for the actions of the first Adam.

On the cross of Calvary, Jesus Christ undid all the evil that the first Adam foisted upon the human race. His cross became the real Tree of Life where we can gain eternal life. As Jesus said, "I am the way, the truth, and the life" (John 14:6). If we "eat of that tree"—accept his sacrifice on it as an act of mercy that redeems us—we, too, can live forever with him. ✦

A STITCH IN TIME

What do you believe about the real Tree of Life—the cross upon which Jesus Christ died? What decision have you made about accepting the sacrifice made at Calvary? What would you like to tell someone else about the eternal life that Jesus promises?

PRAYER

Lord God, thank you for sending Jesus to die for my sins. I thank you also that I will someday go to be with you. Thank you for preparing a place for me.

On Pins and Needles

THE TYPE OF THREAD USED FOR CREWEL IS VERY IMPORTANT. CREWEL IS ACTUALLY A FINE TWO-PLY WOOL. TRUE CREWEL WOOL IS A PRODUCT OF GREAT BRITAIN. MOST OF THE YARN WE BUY THESE DAYS IS REALLY PERSIAN WOOL. YOU CAN DIFFERENTIATE ENGLISH WOOL FROM PERSIAN WOOL BY LOOKING AT A LENGTH OF YARN. ENGLISH WOOL HAS TWO STRANDS AND PERSIAN HAS THREE. PERSIAN WOOL IS OF A ROUGHER TEXTURE THAN BRITISH CREWEL THREADS.

USE PIECES OF YARN ABOUT TWENTY INCHES LONG, BECAUSE THE CONSTANT PULLING OF THE THREAD IN AND OUT OF THE FABRIC CAN WEAR IT OUT. IT WILL BE HELPFUL TO MOVE THE NEEDLE BACK AND FORTH TO A NEW POSITION ON THE YARN TO AVOID WEARING IT OUT IN ONE SPOT. PROFESSIONAL CREWEL WORKERS TWIST THE THREAD AFTER EVERY COUPLE OF STITCHES.

Stuffed Full

If you give, you will receive. Your gift will return to you in full measure, pressed down, shaken together to make room for more, and running over. Whatever measure you use in giving— large or small—it will be used to measure what is given back to you.

LUKE 6:38

Many years ago, just about three months before my son was born, my husband and I were pastoring a very small home missions church. We decided that a missions convention would be good training for this struggling church. The people had never been exposed to the idea of sacrificial giving, so my husband decided we should give to the convention the money we had saved for our son's birth.

I readily agreed. Later, we were invited to speak to a women's gathering in a nearby town. At the end of our speaking, they asked us to leave the room. We couldn't imagine why, until we returned and found they had taken an offering that was—to the penny—the amount we had given away. But there was more. Boxes and boxes of groceries lined the walls. There were gift certificates for clothing and toys for our little girl.

Money and gifts continued to pour in through the holiday season. There was more abundance for this Christmas than we had ever had before. We were stuffed full of good things.

There is a kind of needlework that is stuffed full. It is *trapunto*. Trapunto was first used on the island of Sicily to decorate the garments and furnishings of the wealthy. Several Sicilian trapunto quilts have survived, one from the 1400s.

In traditional quilting, two layers of fabric and a layer of filling are sandwiched together and held in place by tiny stitches. In trapunto quilting, two layers of fabric with no stuffing are quilted together in a design. Then the design is stuffed from the back to give the finished piece an embossed or three-dimensional appearance. If the quilting is done in very narrow lines and stuffed with cords, it is called "Italian quilting."

A modern usage of trapunto is to quilt a preprinted fabric design and stuff it to raise certain portions of the design. To add texture and interest, a number of stitches, embroidery, and attachments can be done on a piece. Portions can then be stuffed to raise or "pop out" a design. Trapunto can be used with appliqué to raise the decorative parts of the design.

Trapunto is lovely on decorative pillows, bedspreads, and pictures for the walls. It is also lovely on clothing. I once made for my mother a floor-length teal-blue skirt and worked a trapunto design that looked like a fleur-de-lis along the bottom. It was elegant.

Trapunto can be done on cotton, linen, wool, organza, or burlap. It provides a great deal of room for creative expression and individuality. It can be plain, fancy, traditional, modern, delicate, or bold.

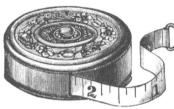

If we were to make trapunto and skimped on the stuffing, we'd have a poor piece of needlework. After all, what you put into something is what you get out of it. In trapunto needlework, if we didn't pay attention to detail and refused to stuff even the tiniest corners, the finished design would be lacking.

Life is the same. What we put into it is what we get out of it. Giving grudgingly reaps a less-than-joyous response. That's why God enables us to be "stuffed full" of his grace in order to be cheerful givers of our time, talents, and resources. Giving from a heart stuffed full of God's love will reap a "stuffed full" response. ❖

A STITCH IN TIME

What are you "stuffed" full of? Good thoughts? Love of the Lord? How can you share your "stuffing" with others? What have others given you that you particularly enjoyed? What do you enjoy giving?

PRAYER

Father, show me ways to give of myself or my resources. Help me, dear Lord, to remember that everything I do, I'm doing for you.

On Pins and Needles

A GOOD FIRST TRAPUNTO PROJECT IS A PILLOW. CUT A TWELVE-INCH SQUARE, CENTERING THE DESIGN YOU WISH TO FEATURE. CUT A BACKING PIECE TO THE SAME SIZE. A LOOSELY WOVEN BACKING WILL ALLOW YOU TO INSERT STUFFING BY PULLING THE THREADS APART WITHOUT CUTTING THE FABRIC. A TIGHTLY WOVEN FABRIC WILL HAVE TO BE CUT TO INSERT THE STUFFING. HAND-QUILT AROUND THE FEATURES OF THE DESIGN YOU WISH TO RAISE. USE TINY STITCHES AND MATCHING THREAD. IF YOU WANT THE STITCHES TO BE PART OF THE DESIGN, USE CONTRASTING THREAD OR METALLIC THREAD. THE QUILTING CAN BE DONE BY SEWING MACHINE IF YOU WISH.

TURN THE PIECE OVER, CUT SLITS, AND STUFF THE DESIGN. STUFF ALL THE WAY TO THE ENDS OF THE DESIGN, USING A SMALL TOOL SUCH AS AN ORANGE STICK OR A NUTPICK.

Cutting Away What's Unnecessary

> *He cuts off every branch that doesn't produce fruit, and he prunes the branches that do bear fruit so they will produce even more. You have already been pruned for greater fruitfulness by the message I have given you.*
>
> **JOHN 15:2-3**

I once moved to a piece of property that had a couple of old apple trees and a pear tree. The first year I lived there, I did nothing with the trees, and the fruit was minimal in size and quality. The next year I had the trees pruned to see what would happen. What happened was a bumper crop of fruit. There was so much fruit, we couldn't eat it all.

There is something about cutting away the extraneous that brings out the best in anything being pruned. This gardening truth also applies to cutwork and to our lives as well.

The very delicate embroidery known as cutwork cuts away large pieces of fabric to reveal openwork designs. It requires only one stitch—the buttonhole stitch. It has a delicate look, almost of lace, but is a very sturdy embroidery. Because there is only one stitch used, it is easy to learn. However, cutwork, to be beautiful, must be carefully worked and can be somewhat tedious.

To do a cutwork piece, first trace the pattern you have chosen onto the fabric. Then outline the pattern in running stitch to stabilize and mark the design. Next cover the running stitch in closely worked buttonhole stitch. The ridge formed by the buttonhole stitch should be toward the area of design that will be cut away.

When you have finished working buttonhole stitch all around the design area, use embroidery scissors to cut away the interior area of the design. Work from the wrong side and cut close to the base of the stitches, without cutting into the stitches themselves. When you turn the piece over, you will see that you have created a lovely lacy effect.

That's all there is to cutwork. If the areas you cut away are very large, however, the design will sag. When that happens, you have to fill that area with bridges of worked bars. These become a part of the intricate design.

The need for bars has to be thought through before you begin doing any work on the piece. When you are doing the outline running stitches in the beginning and come to an area that will need a bar, carry the yarn across the area, take a small stitch, bring the yarn back and take another stitch where you started. Then work back across the threads with buttonhole stitch. When the bar is complete, continue the outline-stabilizing running stitch. Continue on to the next area that will need a bar and repeat the process, so that the bars are put in and

worked in buttonhole stitch before any fabric is cut away—in fact, before any buttonhole stitch is worked to outline the pattern.

It is the cutting away of excess fabric that causes the beauty of cutwork to be seen. If you don't cut away the fabric, you just have buttonhole-stitch embroidery on fabric. But when you trim the excess, you reveal the beauty of the cutwork.

God also does this with us. Once in a while he cuts away attitudes we can do without, attitudes we often struggle with. These include the "I can't do its," the "I'll never make its," and the "it's hopeless" thoughts. Procrastination urges are also purged, making room for the steady growth of persistence.

Pruning a tree helps it produce the best fruit. Pruning roses and getting rid of fading blossoms gives us a continual supply of beautiful flowers. Trimming away unnecessary words makes a piece of writing better. Cutting away the excesses of our lives allows the beauty of our character to be seen—the godly character the Master Designer intended in us. ❖

A STITCH IN TIME

What is there in your life that needs to be cut away to make room for new growth? Sometimes we think that God's cutting is an act of cruelty—that he doesn't want us to be happy. But the truth is, he wants us to thrive, to be as beautiful as we can be.

PRAYER

All right, Father. Take the sharp scissors of your Word and "prune" me. Thank you for the love you have for me—love that allows me to grow in you.

On Pins and Needles

You might look for cutwork pieces in antique shops that specialize in antique linens. After you are more aware what good, handmade cutwork looks like, you can begin to watch at garage sales and in thrift shops for pieces to use as designs or just to grace your home.

If those old cutwork pieces are damaged, you can repair them using the buttonhole stitch and bars. Some of the designs you will find are incredibly beautiful and intricate. From these old designs you can make patterns to be used on new linens.

When you think about doing cutwork, be sure to choose a fabric that won't fray.

A Study in Patience

Knowing God leads to self-control. Self-control leads to patient endurance, and patient endurance leads to godliness. Godliness leads to love for other Christians, and finally you will grow to have genuine love for everyone.

2 PETER 1:6-7

They swish across the ice in a stunning display of grace and power, these champion ice skaters, and part of our fascination with them is the beautiful costumes they wear and the appropriateness of those costumes to the music and theme of the performance. Often those costumes are beaded and extremely ornate.

A friend used to make skating costumes for ice skaters and knew that every bead had to be stitched securely in place. Just imagine what might happen if at some crucial moment, a bead—or several—popped off and rolled across the ice. Imagine the break in concentration for the skater. Imagine the possibility of injury if that bead got between the skater's blade and the ice.

My friend would sit for hours stitching tiny beads onto costumes.

Carefully, and with great patience, she attached them to the costume, bringing great beauty to the design of the garment.

Beadwork is a pleasant mix of craft and stitchery and has been used to decorate the costumes of mankind since the earliest times, when men attached shells and crude beads cut from bone and stone. Beadwork was used to identify those of distinctive roles like chieftains and leaders. Beads traveled across oceans in the holds of ships as valued items of trade and were a primary source of exchange with Native Americans in the early days of our country. Those Native Americans became unbelievably skilled in applying beads to clothing and other decorative items.

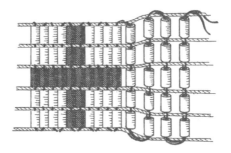

Beadwork is among the first crafts a child learns as he or she strings large wooden beads on a shoelace. The prayer memory device of the rosary is nothing more than beadwork.

But the stringing and attachment of tiny glass beads and pearls is an art form that requires much patience. And patience is a virtue that we as Christians are encouraged to pursue. The word patience means endurance. Endurance sounds so hard, until we realize that just like attaching beads to a garment, we don't have to do it all at once. We attach beads to a garment one at a time. And we don't have to have endurance or patience all at once. We gain it slowly by trusting God one step at a time.

We are to run with patience—endurance—the race that is set before us (Hebrews 12:1). No race was ever won in a single leap. It takes putting one foot in front of the other, over and over, until we cross the finish line. And it is the trying of our faith that brings endurance (James 1:3). So when the hard times come, we just keep putting one foot in front of the other until one day we realize we have learned

patience and endurance.

So we sew on one bead, we endure one test, we learn to love one unlovable person, and we attach patience to our lives.

Whether we are creating costumes for those who spin across the ice or simply living a quiet, enduring, faithful life, we are creating something of lasting beauty. ✣

A STITCH IN TIME

What are the times when you feel most in need of patience? What has helped you to endure in the past? How has God tested your faith?

PRAYER

Holy Spirit, teach me to be patient. Walk beside me and give me faith so that my patience may be perfected. Help me to know you, to really know you.

On Pins and Needles

Use a long, thin needle for beadwork. These needles are very fine and flexible and about the same size at the hole as they are at the point. The holes in many beads are too small for most regular needles. You may also want to gather several beads on a needle at one time before stitching them down.

Use thread that is strong enough to carry the weight of the beads. One that is recommended is Gutermann Polytwist.

Beeswax can be a great aid in keeping long pieces of thread from tangling. Run the thread through the beeswax a couple of times.

Of utmost importance is a container for your beads. Many beads are purchased in plastic boxes with lids, but a container with many compart- ments is helpful in quickly finding the beads you wish to use.

Pass It On

*Let each generation tell its children of your
mighty acts. . . . Everyone will share the story
of your wonderful goodness; they will sing with
joy of your righteousness.*

PSALM 145:4, 7

Grandma, where does the moon go in the daytime?"

"It doesn't go anywhere, Sandra. Sometimes you can see the moon
in the daytime, and sometimes it's on the other side of the earth."

"Is there really a man in the moon?"

"Not really."

"Could I ever live on the moon?"

"Maybe someday."

"Grandma, do I ask too many questions?"

It was a good question, for three-year-olds can ask as many as three
hundred questions a day.

Grandma answered, "No, Sandra, you don't ask too many questions.
That's how you learn."

Grandma thought about her conversation with Sandra as she sat down
to work smocking on a dress for her. *Smocking is like answering Sandra's*

questions, she thought. *You take a pinch here and a pinch there and pull it all together to make this lovely dress. You answer a question here and you answer a question there, and soon you have a beautiful life with values and integrity.*

When I think of smocking, I think of little girls in English gardens wearing delicate smocked dresses and big straw hats, and carrying baskets of flowers.

Smocking is a type of embroidery that both decorates and gathers the fabric at the same time. It is worked from a series of dots laid out in a grid fashion. Patterns for smocking can be purchased and transferred to the fabric, or you can simply grid your own smocking. Checks and stripes provide a readymade grid.

There are two kinds of smocking: English and "regular." English smocking is considered easier than "regular" smocking. In English smocking the dots are transferred to the wrong side of the fabric. Then long running stitches are made from dot to dot across each line of the grid. The running stitches are pulled up to gather the fabric before smocking stitches are done on the right side of the fabric.

There are a number of other decorative smocking stitches, none of which are difficult to learn, and any good needlework book should give you a wide selection of these. If smocking is worked on a baby christening gown, the dress could well become an heirloom—an item you will pass down from one generation to the next.

There is something else that God wants us to pass on: the truth about the love of a Father for a lost world, about our ability to live triumphantly regardless of our circumstances. It is the duty of older genera-

tions to tell the next about God and how he wants us to live. "Let each generation tell its children of your mighty acts. . . . Everyone will share the story of your wonderful goodness; they will sing with joy of your righteousness" (Psalm 145:4, 7).

In Deuteronomy, we're told to "repeat [these commands] again and again . . . when [we] are at home and . . . away on a journey, when . . . lying down and when . . . getting up again" (6:7).

So when you are smocking a baby dress for a new granddaughter or to give to the child of a friend, pray into each stitch a little prayer for her. And when you can, pass on to that little one the Good News that Jesus loves her. ❖

A STITCH IN TIME

What would you like to tell the next generation about the love of the Savior? To whom can you pass on the truths about God? What methods would you use to teach others?

PRAYER

Father, how wonderful it is to see children come to know you as their Savior and Lord. Help me to pass on your truths to my family and to others you send my way. May your praise ever be on my lips.

ON PINS AND NEEDLES

SINCE SMOCKING GATHERS FABRIC, REMEMBER YOU'LL NEED A PIECE 2½ TO 3 TIMES WIDER THAN YOU WISH THE FINISHED WORK TO BE.

WHEN CHOOSING FABRICS FOR SMOCKING, CHOOSE THOSE THAT WILL SHIRR (GATHER) WELL. HEAVY, STIFF FABRICS ARE NOT SUITABLE FOR SMOCKING. INSTEAD, CHOOSE LIGHTWEIGHT FABRICS. FOR A FIRST PROJECT YOU MIGHT TRY A CHECKED GINGHAM—THE SQUARES PROVIDE A READYMADE GRID.

IN SMOCKING, A "STEM" OR "OUTLINE" EMBROIDERY STITCH IS WORKED FROM LEFT TO RIGHT (IF YOU ARE RIGHT-HANDED; WORK IT THE OPPOSITE WAY IF YOU ARE LEFT-HANDED). PICK UP ONLY A COUPLE OF THREADS ON THE POINT OF THE NEEDLE. ALWAYS HOLD THE THREAD BELOW THE NEEDLE AS YOU TAKE A STITCH. EACH STITCH ANCHORS A PLEAT AND DECORATES THE SMOCKING AS WELL.

Why Worry? Be Happy!

And why worry about your clothes? Look at the lilies and how they grow. They don't work or make their clothing, yet Solomon in all his glory was not dressed as beautifully as they are. And if God cares so wonderfully for flowers that are here today and gone tomorrow, won't he more surely care for you?

MATTHEW 6:28-30

There is a wonderful, trendy needlework called *ribbon embroidery* (different from ribbon weaving) in which silk or man-made-fiber ribbons are threaded through chenille, embroidery, or tapestry needles and used in a way that would be similar to the use of embroidery floss. The results are stunning—when using silk ribbons, each stitch is much broader and so the work goes faster and there is much more color than when using embroidery floss. It is also possible to make three-dimensional flowers by gathering the ribbon into rosettes and other flower shapes, and by working the ribbons into leaves.

Instead of talking weight of thread, you talk *mms* of ribbon—*mm* standing for millimeter. When working ribbon embroidery, it is also

possible to incorporate bits of old
lace, antique or modern buttons,
pieces of fabric, beads, and other
"findings."

Ribbon embroidery may be one of the
newest techniques among needlework,
but it was first done in the 1920s and fell out
of popularity until just recently. One of the
reasons for its demise after the twenties was that silk ribbons were
rather flimsy. Any garment with silk-ribbon embroidery could not
be washed. But now with the advent of rayon, polyester, and other
man-made fibers, the embroidered object can be laundered and is
more durable. Ribbons come in a wide range of colors. Silk, however,
remains very popular and it, too, is available in literally hundreds
of colors.

One of the nicest things about ribbon embroidery is the speed with
which it can be worked. It doesn't take a lot of ribbon embroidery to turn
a plain-Jane sweater into something very special. There are really only
one or two additional stitches to learn in addition to those you probably
already know for floss embroidery. One is the ribbon stitch, and the
other you may already know because it is used in candlewicking—the
colonial knot.

In looking at the beauty of ribbon embroidery, I could not help but be
reminded of the verse in Matthew that reminds us not to worry about
tomorrow. It tells us that God clothes the lilies. Did you know that the
lilies mentioned here were probably anemones—those beautiful crimson,
purple, pink, velvety-looking flowers that spring from the ugliest little

bulbs you've ever seen? Anemone bulbs look like a small lump of coal, and they are about as hard.

God clothes anemones—the lilies—and I think he did a rather splendid job. Once a few years back, I spent a month in England. I understand now why English print fabrics are full of flowers. I looked  at bright-green grassy meadows "embroidered" with flowers of all kinds and knew that God's handiwork is perfect.

He tells us that if he cares for flowers, which are literally here today and gone tomorrow, he will care for us unendingly. Sometimes the only way we can truly begin to understand that he cares for us is by going through some really deep waters. When we come out the other side of the trial, changed, but intact, we come to understand that he never leaves us nor forsakes us. ❖

A STITCH IN TIME

What are the times you're most tempted to worry? Look back at today's passage (Matthew 6:28-30). How can the truths cited in these verses help you to trust God?

PRAYER

Oh, Father, as we look at a meadow laced with beautiful flowers that came from your creative hand or look at a beautiful newborn child, help us to trust you and to know that, because we are your children, you mean only good for us and never harm.

On Pins and Needles

Use a chenille needle when working with ribbon and lace. A chenille needle will penetrate both the fabric and the lace. When you are making wrapped flowers and colonial knots, however, work them with tapestry needles, since the blunt tip is less likely to snag or pierce the ribbon. In some cases you may want to use an embroidery needle for finer work. You may also want to mix ribbon and floss embroidery in the same piece.

When working a ribbon-work piece, start with the three-dimensional flowers first. Then when you have all of them in place, work around them with the remaining embroidery. Think about adding beads to the center of flowers as an extra touch.

Shadows Aren't Real

Now we see things imperfectly as in a poor mirror, but then we will see everything with perfect clarity. All that I know now is partial and incomplete, but then I will know everything completely, just as God knows me now.

1 CORINTHIANS 13:12

There is a lovely embroidery known as "shadow embroidery." It probably originated in the eighteenth century and was worked with white thread on white translucent fabrics such as organdy, lawn, or batiste.

The embroidery is done mainly from the wrong side of the fabric. Large areas of the design are worked in herringbone stitch on the wrong side. The small stitches, which anchor the herringbone stitches, cause an outline of the design to be formed in a double line of stitches on the right side of the fabric. So now you have herringbones on the backside of the fabric, and a double running stitch line on the front. The crisscrosses of the herringbone provide a shadowy filling of space. Now single stem or outline embroidery is worked on the right side of the fabric over the outlining stitches. Today, shadow embroidery is sometimes worked with colored threads on a wide variety of sheer man-made fabrics as well as white on white.

Shadow embroidery is a great picture of a biblical truth. Sometimes we'd like to know what lies ahead, but God loves us too much to burden us with knowing what the future holds. We could not face it if we knew the sorrow, pain, trials, and temptations that are ahead. We'd want to quit right now. And if he told us of the joys of heaven, we could not understand the magnificence of all that awaits us. So the future remains shadowed for us.

C. S. Lewis, in his book *The Last Battle*, had something to say about this "shadow life":

> You may have been in a room in which there was a window that looked out on a lovely bay of the sea or a green valley that wound away among mountains. And in the wall of that room opposite to the window there may have been a looking glass. And as you turned away from the window you suddenly caught sight of that sea or that valley, all over again, in the looking glass. And the sea in the mirror, or the valley in the mirror, were in one sense just the same as the real ones: yet at the same time they were some-
> how different—deeper, more wonderful, more like places in a story: in a story you have never heard but very much want to know.

Once in a while we get glimpses of what God wants for us,

for both here on earth and after we die and go to live with him. Life in God's kingdom is actually more "real" than the "shadow" life we are  living now. It is deeper and more wonderful than life as we know it. "Now we see things imperfectly as in a poor mirror," as 1 Corinthians 13:12 says. But in heaven, all things will be revealed. We'll see Jesus as he is. We'll understand some of the mysteries that plague us here on earth. This "real life" is the gift God has waiting for us when he at last sweeps away all the shadows and we can see as he sees. ✤

A STITCH IN TIME

What would you like to ask God right now about your life? What are you concerned about in regard to the future? What are your hopes for the future?

PRAYER

Father, it's so easy for me to fret and wonder about the future. I sometimes wonder why you don't give me more clues about the future. Oh, God, help me to see that you have a plan for me. Someday all the shadows will be blown away and I will clearly see your plan.

On Pins and Needles

When using colored thread, select shades that are deeper in hue than the desired finished effect, since the sheer fabric will diffuse the color.

Another idea is to use <u>colored</u> sheer fabric instead of white and then work the embroidery with thread that is even deeper in hue than the colored fabric.

When working with colored thread, you may not want the colored backstitches from the herringbone to be seen on the right side. Cover these with outline or stem stitches in a color of your choice.

In shadow embroidery, no knots or tails must show from the right side of the fabric. Therefore, always leave a tail on a new piece of thread. When you are finished with that thread, go back and thread the tail into the needle and weave it through several herringbone stitches. Trim close to the stitching.

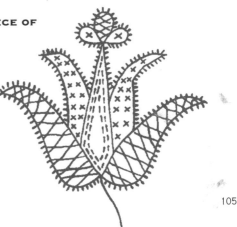

Button, Button, Who's Got the Button?

I recall all you have done, O Lord; I remember your wonderful deeds of long ago. They are constantly in my thoughts. I cannot stop thinking about them.

PSALM 77:11-12

My mother has three or four tin Lipton tea canisters filled with buttons. When I was a child, we always looked through the canisters for buttons to replace lost ones. Now, many years later, these buttons are treasures; perhaps the canisters are too.

A friend once told me that whenever she was sick, out would come her "jewels"—her collection of buttons. She would sort through them and pretend she was a queen sitting among her bed pillows sorting her treasures.

Centuries ago, buttons were used strictly as ornamentation by the Greeks and Romans. The first ones were made of wood, bone, shell, or metal and were carved into geometric shapes. Later, button use became more widespread. There was a certain kind of pride in how many buttons one could place on a garment. In fact, in 1520, King Francis I of France had 13,400 buttons sewn

on a black velvet suit to wear to a meeting with
the king of England. Talk about a power suit!

Button makers can create buttons by
crocheting a small circular floral pattern—
something like a tiny doily—in the size they
need. Patterns for crocheted buttons can be
found in needlework magazines. To complete
the button, they use a running stitch around
the edge of the piece. Since crochet is see-
through, it often requires a circular fabric liner
in a color that matches or contrasts with the
garment. The liner and the crocheted piece
are then worked as one as the button maker
gathers them around the button.

Many of us keep buttons in jars. As we look
at buttons, we remember the people who wore them. An antique button
might remind us of a beloved grandmother. A button shaped like a
slice of watermelon might remind us of a play garment a sister wore
to a picnic.

Remembrances are important. The Bible is a storehouse
of remembrances. Asaph the psalmist wrote, "I recall all
you have done, O Lord; I remember your wonderful deeds
of long ago. They are constantly in my thoughts. I cannot
stop thinking about them" (Psalm 77:11-12). To Asaph, these remembrances of God's mighty deeds were like the treasured buttons in the
Lipton tea canisters.

Remembrances also serve a useful purpose, like a replacement button

does. A remembrance of the way God acted in the past can help a person who is going through a depressing time. He or she could search through his/her "jar" of remembrances and pull out a promise of God's faithfulness. This promise can be used to replace the depressing thoughts.

Maybe we all need to keep a jar full of slips of paper with remembrances of what God has done for us written upon them. Like the writer in the verse above, we will be greatly encouraged if we "cannot stop thinking about" all that he has done. ❖

A STITCH IN TIME

What has God done for you in the last month? in the last year? in your lifetime? You might consider making a "remembrance jar." This could be a list of answered prayers, or a list of things God has done for you, each written on a separate note card.

PRAYER

Dear Father, when I'm tempted to complain that you aren't doing enough for me, help me to stop and remember what you have already done for me. Help me to live my life with gratitude for who you are, more than for what you have done.

On Pins and Needles

You can make decorative needlework buttons to adorn your clothing. They can be completed rather quickly. Purchase one-inch-diameter plastic washers and completely cover the plastic by working buttonhole stitch, using pearl cotton, all the way around the ring.

To make a basketweave button, thread ribbons—the kind used for ribbon embroidery—into a chenille needle. Starting at the outside of your buttonhole-stitched ring, thread the needle through the ridge formed by the buttonhole stitch, then cross to the other side of the ring and take a tiny stitch through the buttonhole ridge there. Return to the starting point to create one pair of warp ribbons. String five pairs of warp ribbons across the button. Then weave six pairs of woof ribbons through the warp. Pierce through the buttonhole stitch ridge each time to secure the ends of the woven ribbon.

Drawn Out

What this means is that those who become
Christians become new persons. They are not
the same anymore, for the old life is gone.
A new life has begun!

2 CORINTHIANS 5:17

Sometimes what makes a piece of needlework beautiful is not what's worked *into* the fabric but what's taken *out*. Such is the case in Italian openwork, which is also called *hemstitching*. Table linens, sheets, handkerchiefs, and other articles with a straight edge can be beautified with hemstitching. It also looks splendid on collar and cuff edges.

Any openwork is best done on an even-weave fabric in which threads can be counted easily and from which threads can easily be pulled out. The piece is tested by pulling some threads, to see if the fabric will make attractive openwork.

Once a needleworker decides on the width of the hemstitching, the threads are pulled to that width. After the threads are drawn, turn the hem and baste the edge very close to the pulled threads. Now you are ready to begin hemstitching.

There is one basic stitch, and it is used along the hem side of the drawn threads; or for a more decorative look, it can be used on both sides of the open area. In hemstitching, a small stitch is taken at the edge of the hem to anchor the thread. Then the needle is passed under a group of four to six threads and moved to the right over the top of the threads. On a second pass downward, the needle is inserted into the first thread of the fabric above the opening. Pulling the stitch tight forms the bundle. This process is repeated until all of the threads are drawn into bundles and the hem is secure.

Pulling out the threads makes the piece beautiful. Just imagine what would happen if the needleworker began to pull threads from a length of very fine linen in preparation for hemstitching and the cloth began to clutch at them and yell, "No, I'm not going to let you take away my threads. I've earned them and you can't have them. I want to stay the way I am." Pretty silly, huh?

I can imagine that the needleworker might say, "But I have a plan for you, a plan that will make you so beautiful you will be treasured for years to come. I want you to be the best you can be, and I need to remove these things from you." If the fabric still refused, the needleworker would then have to make something less beautiful. The fabric that may have been intended as an altar cloth for a cathedral might be relegated to the kitchen to wipe pots.

We sometimes question

God's work in our lives. Yet we are the fabric the Master Designer longs to form into a beautiful, creative design. It's often the removal of bad attitudes, bad habits, and sinful actions that gives God a chance to make something beautiful of us. This starts through a relationship with Jesus. Our old ways of doing things are "cut away." "A new life has begun!" as 2 Corinthians 5:17 joyously proclaims. We are drawn out of our old ways of thinking into the mind-of-Christ way of thinking. ❖

A STITCH IN TIME

What do you see that God has drawn out of your life? What has God placed into your life? What do you like best about your walk with God? How is your new life in Christ different from your old life?

PRAYER

Oh, Father, there are so many ways that I might have clutched at things you have asked me to relinquish. Maybe I've held on to relationships about which you've said, "Give them to me." Perhaps I've ignored attitudes that I know displease you. I need you to help me to surrender all of my life to you.

On Pins and Needles

As you think about your piece, decide early on which kind of corner you want. When you are selecting threads to pull, the kind of corner you want will determine how you pull the threads at the corners.

If you choose an overlapped hem, pull the threads all the way to the edge of the fabric. This will form a square in the corner with hemstitching on either side. In a mitered corner, where the openwork turns the corner, cut the threads at the place where the hemstitching turns the corner.

When you do the hemstitching stitch over a bundle of threads, the binding thread may want to slide toward the middle of the bundle. If so, use your fingernail to slide the stitch right up tight against the fabric edge.

What's Down Under Shows Through

You have tested my thoughts and examined my heart in the night. You have scrutinized me and found nothing amiss, for I am determined not to sin in what I say.

PSALM 17:3

J ust look at this needlework. It's so primitive . . . powerful . . . brilliantly colored. What is it?"

We were viewing a display of needlework that made the gallery walls pop with color. "It's San Blas appliqué," my companion said.

"And what, please tell me, is San Blas appliqué?"

"San Blas appliqué is also called reverse appliqué. Its best-known needleworkers are the Cuñas—the native people of the San Blas Islands off the coast of Panama. The technique uses these primitive designs to decorate the *molas*—blouses—of the women. See—" my friend pointed to several pieces—"the motifs mimic animals, plants, and other forms found in nature. And see here, there are slits of colors across the face of the work that give this appliqué its unique look."

"It's beautiful," I concluded.

San Blas or reverse appliqué is worked from the bottom up. The

Cuñas start with the bottom layer. As each layer of fabric is added, they cut and stitch, then add another layer of a different fabric and repeat until all the fabrics have been applied.

Modern cut-through appliqué is much simpler. To do reverse appliqué, all the fabric layers are sandwiched together and basted. Then shapes are cut from the top down to the color of choice. Finally the edges are folded back carefully and stitched with tiny stitches.

The first shape cut through from the top is large enough to accommodate any other shapes and colors that will show in that area. With this in mind, the needleworker must think through the way in which fabric colors are layered. He or she traces the largest pattern on the top piece and, with sharp embroidery scissors, cuts away the fabric inside the tracing to reveal the layer beneath. He or she turns the edge under about ¼ inch and blindstitches it to the layer below without catching the third, fourth, or fifth layers.

Then the process begins for drawing, cutting, trimming, and stitching a design for the next elements on the second, third, fourth, and fifth layers.

People have different layers too. What's down underneath, however, shows through in our attitudes toward each other and toward God. That's why authenticity is such a gift.

Authenticity. What a wonderful word. There are people among us who are authentic—genuine—all the way through. What you see is what they are. When you cut down through the layers of their lives, you find consistent quality and beauty. The deeper you go, the more beautiful they become—like a piece of cut-through, reverse embroidery.

Sometimes we can fool others by only revealing one of our top "layers." We may cover up bad attitudes with another couple of layers.

But God is never fooled by any attempts we make at "the great cover-up." God sees the real deal, warts and all.

How wonderful to be able to echo with David, "You have tested my thoughts and examined my heart in the night. You have scrutinized me and found nothing amiss" (Psalm 17:3). May that ever be true about our lives. ✣

A STITCH IN TIME

What is your description of an authentic life? Take a good look at the authenticity of your own life. When you are cut by the hard times of life, what shows through? When your outer layer is turned back, what lies underneath?

PRAYER

Father God, redo the layers of my life so that when I am bruised or cut by trials, only your beauty shows through. Forgive me for the things I have hidden from others. I know you already know what's under the surface. I long to be authentic in every area of my life so that you will be honored by all I am and all I do.

On Pins and Needles

Fabric for San Blas appliqué should be lightweight, tightly woven, and opaque. Five layers of fabric are the maximum. You'll need matching thread for each color.

Reverse appliqué can be done quite attractively using the sewing machine, working a narrow zigzag or satin stitch around the edge. In this case it is not necessary to turn under the edges. They are completely covered by the machine stitching. If you wish to skip a layer of fabric, straight stitch around the drawn shape. Cut away the shape from the uppermost layers to expose the layer of color you wish to use. Then zigzag over the cut shape to cover the raw edges and the straight stitching.

Mere Gold

*These trials are only to test your faith, to show
that it is strong and pure. It is being tested as
fire tests and purifies gold—and your faith is far
more precious to God than mere gold.*

1 PETER 1:7

Some years ago, it was my privilege to view artifacts of the Incas of
South America. Among the artifacts were vessels and breastplates of
hammered gold—solid gold. They were covered with tooled work, and
filigrees had been soldered on.

However, to me as a needleworker, the most fascinating part of the
exhibit was the garments that incorporated threads of gold. The designs
were exquisite and intricate. The threads of gold were fine, and most
were unbroken. Imagine a king of the Incas coming out of his fortress on
a sunny day wearing a garment of golden threads with a golden helmet
on his head. He must have looked like the sun itself.

As I looked at the exhibit I thought to myself, *These were not primitive
people. This was a highly developed culture with amazing skills. Where did
they learn this? Where did these marvelous designs come from?* I'm not sure
anyone knows the answers to those questions, but as far back as Exodus

in the Bible, people were hammering gold into ultrafine sheets and cutting it into threads for the garments of the priests.

Gold work is luxury work. It has been used for the robes of biblical priests, for ecclesiastical garb, for royal attire, and for court dress. Today it is used only for very exquisite needlework. If you were to gold work a small evening bag or an elegant belt, it would be an heirloom your children would cherish.

Japanese gold threads are the most available and easiest to handle for traditional embroidery. These metallic threads cannot be pulled through the fabric. Gold threads are easily damaged and will tarnish. To further complicate things, they are springy and coil away from the needleworker. They must be couched down. Couching is the process of fastening a thick cord, or in this case the golden threads, by overcasting the thick cord or gold thread with fine matching or contrasting threads.

Gold goes through a purifying process that helps to refine it. God puts his children through a similar refining process. Trials are the tools that God uses to refine us. Job once said, "But he knows the way that I take; when he has tested me, I will come forth as gold" (Job 23:10, NIV). Peter wrote that our faith, after being tested by trials, will outshine "mere gold" (1 Peter 1:7).

The mention of trials sounds a little scary, doesn't it? After all, we all

know the incredible agony Job went through. But God promises, "I will never fail you. I will never forsake you" (Hebrews 13:5). He guarantees 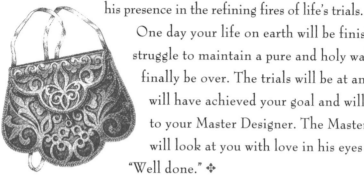 his presence in the refining fires of life's trials.

One day your life on earth will be finished. The struggle to maintain a pure and holy walk will finally be over. The trials will be at an end. You will have achieved your goal and will go at last to your Master Designer. The Master Designer will look at you with love in his eyes and say, "Well done." ✤

A STITCH IN TIME

What trials are you struggling with right now? If your life is currently trial free, how has God helped you in the past? How can you encourage someone who is going through trials right now?

PRAYER

Father, sometimes the trials and testing necessary to bring out gold and to burn away dross in our lives are overwhelming. But you promise that those who endure to the end will receive the crown of life. Help me to endure to the end. Thank you, heavenly Father.

ON PINS AND NEEDLES

FOR GOLD WORK, CHOOSE A HEAVY SILK BROCADE WITH THE PATTERN ALREADY WOVEN IN FOR YOUR FABRIC BASE. THE BROCADE WILL FURTHER ENHANCE THE OVERALL LOOK OF THE GOLD WORK.

PULL THE ENDS OF THE GOLD THREADS THROUGH TO THE BACK-SIDE OF THE PIECE. TO DO THIS, INSERT A LARGE-EYED NEEDLE INTO THE FABRIC FROM THE RIGHT SIDE AND PULL IT THROUGH UNTIL ALL THAT SHOWS IS THE EYE. THEN SLIDE THE GOLD THREAD ENDS INTO THE EYE AND PULL THE ENDS OF THE GOLD THREADS THROUGH THE FABRIC. ANCHOR THE GOLD FROM THE RIGHT SIDE WITH A FEW CLOSE COUCHING STITCHES AT THE POINT WHERE THE NEEDLE WENT DOWN.

IF WORKING WITH REAL GOLD THREADS IS TOO EXPENSIVE, TRY THE NEEDLEWORK USING ORDINARY GOLD-METALLIC THREADS AVAILABLE IN ANY FABRIC STORE.

INDEX OF TOPICS

APPLIQUÉ   46, 83
  San Blas appliqué   114

BANNERS   58

BEADWORK   90

BLACKWORK EMBROIDERY
  54
  Holbein stitch   55
  waste knot   57

BRIDE'S PURSE   42

BUTTONS   106
  buttonhole stitch   109

CARDING WOOL   62
  batts   63

CREWEL EMBROIDERY   78
  English versus Persian wool   81
  Tree of Life   78

CROCHETING   10
  yarn types   13

CUTWORK   86
  buttonhole stitch   86

EMBROIDERY
  blackwork   54
  crewel   78
  cutwork   86

ribbon   98
shadow   102

FINISHING A PIECE   61
  blocking   61
  pressing   61

GOLD WORK   59, 118

HARDANGER NEEDLEWORK
  34
  Kloster blocks   35

HEMSTITCHING   110

JACOBEAN EMBROIDERY
  (see *Embroidery, crewel*)

KNITTING   14
  Aran sweaters   14
  stitches   14, 15

LACEMAKING   66
  bobbins   66

LEFT-HANDED TECHNIQUES
  61, 97

MACRAMÉ   50

PINEAPPLES IN NEEDLEWORK
  74

QUILTING   2, 62
  fabric   2, 5

patterns   3

recycling wool   62

RIBBON EMBROIDERY   98

using a chenille needle   101

using silk ribbons   99

RUG MAKING   22, 26

braid clip   25

braided rugs   22

fabrics   22, 25, 26

hooked rugs   26

SAMPLER   38

SHADOW EMBROIDERY   102

SMOCKING   94

stem embroidery stitch   97

using running stitches   95

TAPESTRIES   18

needles   21

TRAPUNTO   83

WEAVING   30

ribbon   70, 109

warp   30, 109

woof   30, 109

WHITEWORK   6

stitches   7, 9